The Power
of a Promise Kept

The Power
of a Promise Kept

Life Stories by Gregg Lewis

PUBLISHING

Colorado Springs, Colorado

Library of Congress Cataloging-in-Publication Data
Lewis, Gregg A.
    The power of a promise kept: life stories/ by Gregg Lewis.
        p. cm.
    ISBN 1-56179-350-7
    1. Men—Religious life.   2. Christian life.   I. Title.
BV4528.2.L48   1995
248.8'42—dc20   95-6366
                                                          CIP

Front cover design: David Riley & Associates
Front cover illustration: Tom Clark

Printed in the United States of America
95 96 97 98 99/10 9 8 7 6 5 4 3 2 1

Contents

Introduction:
The Power of a Promise Kept

This may be the most unusual book you've ever read.

Its 13 stories are not about sports heroes or superstar entertainers. You'll find no *Fortune* 500 CEOs revealing their secrets of success. Instead, these stories are about men just like you. On the outside, they look like so many individuals you find in church, at work, or in your neighborhood. They have families, careers, and dreams. But they all know their lives aren't perfect, though most have never told anyone their secret fears.

They desire a deep friendship with another man, but they don't know how to start the process.

They try to balance their priorities, but they feel trapped by circumstances they can't change.

They want deeper relationships with their fathers and children, but they don't know how to break negative patterns of communication.

They face tough decisions of conscience and feel they have no one with whom they can confide.

They muddle through marriage knowing their wives are unhappy, but they don't know what to do about it.

They think about the bigger questions of life, like "Why am I here?" but are too busy to search for the answers.

Now, you probably don't fit all those generalizations, but we'd guess you identify with one or more and could no doubt expand the list. That's why

1

this book was written for you—to help real men, who are living life in the trenches, raise the standard.

We doubt you want to stay where you are. You want to be a better man of God. You want to be known more as a man of integrity. You want to grow in your ability to meet the needs of those who are important to you. And whether you're married or single, you want to make a lasting difference in the world.

But where do you start? You begin with some basic promises. We suggest seven:

> 1. I will honor Jesus Christ through prayer, worship, and obedience to His Word in the power of the Holy Spirit.

> 2. I will pursue vital relationships with a few other men, understanding that I need brothers to help me keep my promises.

> 3. I will practice spiritual, moral, ethical, and sexual purity.

> 4. I will build a strong marriage and family through love, protection, and biblical values.

> 5. I will support the mission of my church by honoring and praying for my pastor and by actively giving my time and resources.

> 6. I will reach beyond any racial and denominational barriers to demonstrate the power of biblical unity.

> 7. I will help influence my world, being obedient to the Great Commandment (Mark 12:30-31) and the Great Commission (Matt. 28:19-20).

Those seven simple commitments take a lifetime to live out. We covered the promises in-depth in the book *Seven Promises of a Promise Keeper*. This book is the next step. We want you to see what it looks like when men seek to live out those promises. We want you to see that it's a process, at times a struggle. But it's worth it, because along the way you will find answers to your deepest needs as a man.

Theologians call this process "progressive sanctification." That's a heavy-duty term that is simply expressed in Romans 8:29: "For from the very beginning God decided that those who came to him . . . should become like his Son, so that his Son would be the First, with many brothers" (TLB). In other words, as Christians, we're supposed to become more and more like Jesus Christ.

Now note: That doesn't mean you become perfect overnight. You know from experience that that isn't the case. Positive change takes time. It's a growth process. Sometimes we take one step backward for every two steps forward. But no positive step is too small, and God's intention is clear. If you commit to Him, He will transform you.

Second, you'll have ups and downs. Sometimes you'll fail. None of us likes to fail, but it happens. So when you fail, get back up and keep moving toward becoming all God wants you to be. Some of you may feel you've made too many mistakes to ever recover. Perhaps you messed up a marriage and it cost you a divorce. Or maybe you got fired from a job, betrayed a friendship, or were caught breaking the law and had to serve some time. But we want you to remember that it's never too late to start over. God loves to give His children another chance.

And third, don't try to make lots of major changes all at once. One small step of faith and obedience at a time will lead to the goal of becoming like Christ. We hope this book will help you identify and make those small steps. Realize, too, that all changes—even good ones—create tension in the home. Be patient and allow your family to get used to the difference in you; they'll need time to become convinced that the changes will last.

Now a word about how this book works. The stories are real-life case studies that show how (and how not) to apply the truths of God's Word. At the end of each (and occasionally in the middle), we'll ask you questions to help you evaluate your own life. At the end of each chapter are further questions for group study. Although you can certainly read this book on your own, the greatest benefit will come when you discuss these stories and questions in the context of a small group of men.

But we also need to warn you that there are some surprises. In three cases, we've removed the ending of the story so you don't know what happens. This is so you will honestly wrestle with the issues involved.

And remember, the journeys of the men in this book will be different from your own. We know not every story has a happy ending, at least from a human perspective. You may try to reconcile a relationship and be rejected. You may do the right thing and feel you're being punished for taking a stand. In these stories, we encourage you to dig for the principles. Discover the promises these men made, and realize that God will honor these commitments even if some around you don't understand.

Also, note how in nearly every story, one or more men came alongside the man you're reading about. The point is that we can't go it alone. We need help. We need brothers to encourage us, confront us, and hold us accountable. When Christian brothers come together in meaningful relationship, the burdens they have are no longer so heavy. And the commitments they make are not so intimidating. The fact is, if you want to become all God wants you to be, you need at least one other Christian brother to help you get there.

We believe God wants to raise up ordinary men, men who raise the standard of God's Word, keep their promises, and in the process become *extra-ordinary*. There will be a price to pay, but there will also be great benefits. The 13 stories you'll read here are of men who have raised the standard in their lives. They've made their promises and kept them even when it cost a lot. Some of them, though, have had to face the pain of breaking their promises. It wasn't easy. There has been a lot of struggle, and the struggles continue. But God has honored their perseverance and lifelong commitment, and He will also honor yours.

That's what we mean by the power of a promise kept.

Finally, a word of thanks to the team of Promise Keepers who are responsible for the shape of this book and who wrote the chapter introductions, personal evaluations, group discussion questions, and "My Response" sections for each chapter. That advisory board was made up of mostly Promise Keepers staff and included John Allen, manager of research; Dr. Rod Cooper, national director of educational ministries; Dr. Gordon England, national director of prayer and evangelism; Jim Gordon, manager of publications; Dr. Gary Oliver, board member; Pete Richardson, vice president of communication services; Dr. E. Glenn Wagner, vice president of ministry advancement; David R. White, special assistant to the vice president of communication services; Al Janssen, director of book publishing, Focus on the Family; and Larry Weeden, book editor, Focus on the Family.

God bless you as you make use of this book.

Randy Phillips
President
Promise Keepers

CHAPTER 1

Introduction

It's easy for what we believe to influence what we do on Sunday. The real issue is what difference our faith makes on Monday morning. There are many situations and circumstances where "the Christian thing to do" is blatantly clear. It's always wrong to lie, to cheat, to steal, to bear false witness. But what do we do when faced with a situation where there's no clear teaching of Scripture to guide us? Are we left to float adrift? Do we toss a coin and ask God to guide it to heads or tails?

Our society is walking down a deadly path of moral relativism. All values are at best negotiable and at worst nonexistent. Every day we're influenced by the philosophy and values of those around us. And as Christian men, it's possible to become numb to that relativistic influence without even noticing it. Even many godly pastors, seminary professors, and respected leaders—not to mention businessmen, mechanics, engineers, and other laymen—have not realized the small, subtle changes taking place in their own lives. As a result, they've gotten themselves into serious trouble. They didn't intend to. They didn't ever think it could happen to them. But it did.

If it's your desire to become a Promise Keeper, you need to ask yourself, "Do I understand the importance of moral and ethical purity?" In His teaching, Jesus made a direct connection between Christianity and morality. Who we are should have a direct impact on what we do. The Bible commands us to become "holy and blameless" (Eph. 1:4), to "live a life worthy of the calling you have received" (Eph. 4:1), to be "mature" men (Eph. 4:13), "imitators of God" (Eph. 5:1), to "keep yourself pure" (1 Tim. 5:22) and to "keep oneself from being polluted by the world" (James 1:27).

What do you think of when you hear the word holy? Most of us think of someone other than ourselves. In both Hebrew and Greek, the original languages of the Old and New Testaments, the word refers to something or someone set apart for God. One of the major characteristics of a holy man is purity. Something that is pure is spotless, stainless, free from what weakens or pollutes, free of moral fault. That's our calling.

A Promise Keeper Strives for Ethical Integrity

uppose you're in charge of the biggest project in your company's history, and due to factors beyond your control, things aren't going as well as everyone would like. To obscure that fact, you're asked to play accounting games. Failure to do so might cost your company the contract and could cost you your job. What course would you choose?

That's the kind of dilemma Jeff Vaughn faced a few years ago. After attending a weekend conference in 1993, he told Promise Keepers about that struggle he had encountered in applying his faith to his responsibilities at a leading aerospace company. What was for him a very personal dilemma had national implications for a multibillion-dollar project his company was working on for the federal government. But to fully understand and appreciate Jeff's commitment to being a man of integrity at work, it's helpful to get a little perspective on his personal and professional background.

When Jeff and Sheila Vaughn met and married more than 15 years ago, they brought five kids and a full load of emotional baggage into their relationship—his second marriage, her third. Within a year, they were having serious marital problems of their own. Sheila admits they were quickly learning that "passion and love were not enough to hold a marriage together. We had no solid foundation to build on."

Spiritually, the Vaughns were adrift. Jeff says he was "a backslidden and very carnal Christian." Despite a fairly religious upbringing, Sheila says, "I never heard, or at least never understood, the basic plan of salvation."

But one day a colleague at work, where Sheila was fast ascending the corporate ladder, told her some of his testimony. Perhaps because she was experiencing such turmoil in her marriage, she listened and then began to ask questions. "All my life I'd been searching for answers," she says. "Suddenly, what he was saying filled in all the blanks."

Excited by what she'd heard, Sheila went home to tell Jeff about this new spiritual understanding. And because her co-worker had invited her to visit his church, the Vaughns went the next Sunday morning. At the end of the worship service, when an invitation was given, Sheila went forward to accept Jesus Christ as her personal Savior. Jeff went with her and rededicated his life to the Lord.

"Suddenly I was an on-fire young Christian," Sheila remembers. "I could no longer think about leaving Jeff; I was stuck with him. Seeing no alternative, I got down on my knees and begged God to give us back our marriage."

Jeff says, "She asked for my forgiveness. I asked for hers. And we determined together that with God's help, we would make our marriage work."

"And it has," Sheila adds. "If you talk to anyone who knows us, they'll tell you that after all this time, we still act like newlyweds."

Not that everything changed overnight. The Vaughns admit it has been a process. They've had and continue to have their share of ups and downs. "If I think back 15, 12, even 10 years ago and then look at where I am today," Jeff says, "I can't help thinking, *Wow! How did I ever get from there to here?*" That encouraging sense of progress and growth not only applies to the Vaughns' marriage, but also to other areas of life, like Jeff's job.

Almost all the business done by Jeff's company is with the government—either contracting directly with one of the branches of the military, NASA, or another federal agency, or subcontracting some part of a project being done by one of the larger aerospace firms. Every program handled by his company is assigned a management team whose job it is to oversee the fulfillment of the contract. Jeff, as one of those executives, is responsible for cost and schedule management. "In other words," he explains, "it's my job to make sure my company delivers whatever piece of hardware or software we're developing to our client on schedule and for the price specified in our contract."

Part of the challenge of managing such long-term, multimillion-dollar contracts is keeping up with the constant changes in specifications and plans being made by the client's engineers or at the whim of politicians who ultimately control the purse strings of any government project. So Jeff not only has to monitor his own company's work on a project, but he also has to serve as a liaison—keeping the client updated on his company's progress and keeping his company aware of the client's changing demands. This liaison role requires extensive interaction with the client's representatives through management reviews, progress reports, briefings, and on-site inspections.

For several years, Jeff was assigned to his company's part of the space-station program. While his firm wasn't contracted directly with NASA, the subcontracted project he helped oversee was to mean 10 years of work and hundreds of millions of dollars. The total space-station program added up to billions of dollars a year for all the companies involved. "Our portion was the biggest contract our firm had ever had," Jeff says.

Any government project that big becomes a political issue. Funding is always debated. And if the program falls behind schedule or unexpected cost overruns occur, both political supporters and political opponents begin applying pressure. While that pressure usually starts at the top, it's quickly felt all the way down the line. Since Jeff was his company's man overseeing costs and scheduling, much of the pressure would land squarely on his back.

That's just what happened, because the space-station program was the most challenging and troublesome project Jeff and his company had ever tackled. The sheer size of the overall program and the multitude of subcontractors involved made logistics difficult enough. To complicate things even further, constant engineering changes by NASA and higher-level contractors resulted in literally hundreds of contract changes for Jeff's company. And Jeff, whose job it was to monitor every change so costs and schedule could be adjusted accordingly, was sometimes months and hundreds of contract changes behind because his company's client wasn't communicating those changes in a timely manner.

"It was a logistical and managerial nightmare," he says.

What routinely happens in such programs is that contractors seldom acknowledge cost overruns during the early years. Instead, for example, a contractor given an annual budget of $100 million to provide this and that will issue reports indicating it did, indeed, spend no more than the budgeted $100 million to provide this and *some* of that—with the rest of "that" now scheduled to come out of next year's $100 million budget. But then, unless costs can be cut somewhere else (which is very unlikely), a snowball effect kicks in, and something else has to be pushed to the following year to allow for the conclusion of the previous year's goals. If that pattern continues, the hidden problem gets bigger and bigger until the truth finally comes out. And by then, everyone usually has too much invested to abandon the project, so all that can be done is to appropriate additional funds for the remaining years of the program or extend the project a few years (which amounts to the same thing).

This is just what happened with NASA's massive space-station program. "Every year I was on the program, we fought a constant battle, because of the continuous changes, to live within the funding for the year and to deliver what we'd promised on schedule," Jeff says. "The pressure came right down the line from NASA to our client and all the other contractors. If everyone didn't deliver everything we were supposed to deliver at the cost we had contracted for, not only would we look bad, but our client and its client would look bad all the way up to NASA. And then, when Congress scrutinized NASA's budget, if the program looked as though it had serious overrun problems, the politicians might well terminate the entire project. That would mean not only billions of dollars a year to corporate America, but also thousands of jobs in our company and throughout the entire aerospace industry."

Jeff admits, "I lost a lot of sleep trying to figure out how our company was going to do what we'd contracted to do."

Jeff wrestled with just what to tell his superiors, because he knew they wouldn't like the unvarnished truth.

He eventually concluded it simply couldn't be done—that there were going to be cost overruns. Then he wrestled with just what to tell his superiors, because he knew they wouldn't like the unvarnished truth. Ultimately, however, as a Christian and a man of integrity, Jeff decided that was the only way to go. But when he turned in his conclusions, he received intense pressure to manipulate his figures.

One of his bosses called Jeff into his office and said, "You can't tell me that you can sit here and know for a fact that we can't make up enough ground in the remaining years of this program to meet our delivery schedule. Surely you have to admit there's a chance we can deliver on time."

Jeff admitted he couldn't say with certainty what would happen five years down the road. "But the possibility is very, very slim," he maintained. "And based on my evaluation, I feel there is no way we can fulfill the contract."

Despite that kind of pressure from within his own company, Jeff felt he had no choice but to be just as honest with his company's client—who was no more eager than his bosses to face the truth. "When I presented my revised annual cost figures during a three-day, year-end review at our client's head-quarters," he says, "one of their executives told our team, 'If you guys can't do better than that, you may as well turn in your badges and go home right now. These numbers will never fly with NASA.'"

Jeff and the rest of his team retreated to a conference room to rehash their projected numbers. In time, they all agreed there was no way to do the contracted work for less money. So when the team leader argued for the usual postpone-some-of-the-work-to-a-later-date trick, the team finally agreed— but only after Jeff and others who backed him insisted on being completely open with the client. They would agree to the original amount of funding budgeted as long as they spelled out in careful, written detail what parts of the contract could not be fulfilled or would have to be delayed until the following fiscal year.

As a man of integrity, Jeff says, "I had an obligation to my company and our client to make sure they clearly understood my position—that we could no longer expect to do what we'd promised on the schedule or at the cost we'd agreed to when we signed the original contract. I had to do what I thought was right. And it was up to my superiors, our client, and ultimately their clients to decide what to do with the information I provided."

Someone somewhere made the decision to continue hiding the truth about cost overruns. But the whole thing blew wide open the following year, and Congress held hearings, calling in NASA officials and executives from numerous contractors and subcontractors. As a result, the entire space-station program was scaled back and restructured to include a new partnership with the Russians. In the process, several companies, including Jeff's, lost huge contracts. Many jobs were lost, including those of some of Jeff's superiors. But he was transferred to another team overseeing the cost and scheduling management of one of his company's contracts with the Pentagon.

Jeff will never know for sure, but his carefully documented insistence on honestly reporting his company's part of the space-station program may be one reason he's closing in on a 25-year pin while so many in his industry are out of work. "God has been good," he says. "And I now sleep better than ever."

Personal Evaluation

If you, like Jeff Vaughn, were pressured by your superiors to tell less than the whole truth to a customer, how do you think you would respond? Why? Besides your wife, with whom could you share this? Whom could you ask for help?

A Promise Keeper Strives for Ethical Integrity, Part 2

H ave you ever been treated unfairly by a boss and found yourself hoping for a chance to get revenge? How far do you go in making a case for yourself when your reputation and career may be at risk? And what if that opportunity for revenge arises? How does a Promise Keeper apply a biblical standard in such a case?

Harvey Mitchell had spent more than 10 productive years in the Air Force moving steadily up the promotion ladder. He was consistently honored for excellence in the performance of his duties and universally respected by both superiors and subordinates for his caring Christian character and personal and professional integrity. Then a storm of controversy descended out of nowhere, catching him by surprise and threatening to destroy everything for which he had worked.

Sergeant Harvey Mitchell served as an instructor supervisor in a Fundamental Electronics school—one of more than 60 specialty training schools—on his base. Ten instructors reported directly to him as second in command to the school's top administrator.

Before being promoted to this post, Harvey had himself been an instructor and specialist in electronic weapons technology for the F-16 aircraft. His expertise had been so widely recognized that he'd regularly served as an official Air Force liaison to the engineering departments and factories at manufacturers like Honeywell and General Dynamics.

While teaching in the F-16 school, Harvey received numerous honors, the most prestigious of which was being singled out from hundreds of instructors in all the schools as his base's "instructor of the year."

"I really enjoyed my job," Harvey says. "I loved working with young people, walking into a classroom and taking students from the known to the unknown. I loved watching the light come on in their eyes when they began to grasp some new theory and see practical applications of what I was teaching. I found special joy encouraging and helping students who were struggling with professional and personal problems."

Harvey so enjoyed the teaching role that in his off hours, he coached one of the base's basketball teams and also worked with the chaplain's office to teach a course called "Practical Christian Living." As Harvey explains, "Over the years of growing as a Christian, that was what I'd come to see as my own personal mission—trying to apply my faith and the Word of God in practical ways in my everyday experience."

By all accounts, Harvey did a good job of that. All his students and co-workers realized he was a Christian. And after he accepted a part-time assistant pastor's position with a church in a nearby community, Harvey began to see ways in which his military duties as instructor, counselor, and encourager of young people could be a natural extension of his personal witness and pastoral ministry.

He set a tone in class as an instructor and then as a supervisor that was not only noticed, but also respected. "For example," says Harvey, "I didn't make a big deal of it, but anyone who knew me for very long understood my feelings about profanity. If I walked into a conversation where one of my instructors was angry and swearing about some student, the conversation would come to an embarrassed halt, and the instructor would invariably apologize to me."

Then the higher-ups brought in a new top administrator for the Fundamental Electronics school. Sergeant John Sherman had been a hotshot administrator over at Strategic Air Command (SAC). Morale ran high among his men, and his former school had received the highest ratings on its base. The expectation was that he would provide a real shot in the arm for Fundamental Electronics.

"Sergeant Sherman," recalls Harvey, "was an old-line military man, what we called 'a throwback to the brown shoe days.' He walked into his first meeting with me and the other instructor supervisor with a John Wayne swagger. Stocky and well-built, his very manner fairly shouted, 'I'm the man!' When he entered a room, there was no doubt about who was in control.

"He started out sharing his vision with us—the way a football coach might talk at halftime with his team two touchdowns behind. He told us what blankety-blank problems we were going to tackle first, what blankety-blank steps he wanted to implement, and how we would blankety-blank well get on board his program if we wanted to ride with him to the top. If we didn't, we'd better plan on getting out of the blankety-blank way or we'd get run over, because he planned to do with our school exactly what he'd done in his former school over at SAC."

Harvey didn't mind the gung-ho, you'd-better-be-ready-to-follow-me-or-else attitude. There were plenty of men like that in the military; some of them made very effective commanders. So Harvey was willing to give the guy a chance. But after working so hard to set a Christian tone among the school's staff, Harvey was bothered by the man's steady stream of profanity. When that first meeting was over, Harvey asked to speak to his new boss alone. He told Sergeant Sherman, in as polite and pleasant a way as he could, that while he intended to do whatever he could to help win Fundamental Electronics the highest rating of any school on base, he didn't need the added motivation of profanity in order to do his job.

Sherman responded far better than Harvey feared he might. "No problem," he said. "You have a fine record, Mitchell. People have told me a lot of great things about you. I know you were 'instructor of the year'; you're practically a legend around here. I'm sure you and I will be able to work together just fine. And I'll try to watch my mouth."

And maybe he did try. But profanity was such a part of his nature that trying to curb the habit cramped his style. Within weeks, unbeknownst to Harvey, Sherman went to his own superiors, Major Zylinski and Colonel Webb, to express his feelings of frustration. "You brought me in here to improve this school," he told them. "I intend to do that. But to be successful, I've got to be myself and do things my way. And I've got this guy who is making that difficult . . ."

One day not long after that, Sergeant Sherman called Harvey into his office and asked, "Harv, how much do you know about StanEval [Standardization Evaluation]?"

Harvey shrugged and answered, "I know they work for the general. They're the outfit that comes in every year to inspect our entire program. They usually tear us apart."

"Yeah, that's right," Sherman said with a nod. "Did you know working with StanEval really looks good on a guy's record—a real feather in the old cap?"

"Never thought of that," Harvey replied, wondering where this conversation was going.

"It's true," his boss said. "And I've just learned they need a temporary augmentee over in StanEval. It's just a six-week assignment. They'd like someone from our group. I know you'd do a good job. What would you think about taking it?"

"I've got a lot of things I really would like to get done around here," Harvey said.

"Yeah, sure. But would you give it some thought?"

"Okay," Harvey said.

The next morning, he found a message on his desk telling him to report to StanEval the following Monday. No further dialogue about his feelings. That may have been just as well, however, because Harvey admits, "I wasn't at all happy about my orders!"

He reported as ordered the following week to StanEval at the headquarters of the center commander, a two-star general. There Harvey learned he'd be a member of a crack team of inspectors, each a top expert in his field, who were responsible for keeping the general apprised of the condition of his entire command. In addition to doing regular inspections of the more than 60 training schools on base, the StanEval team inspected 10 geographically separated units stationed throughout the country and overseas. It was, indeed, a high privilege to be assigned to such a respected (and feared) team. For no matter what unit, group, school, or office he walked into, every member of the StanEval team was accorded the honor and authority of the general he represented.

Because of his background in training, Harvey Mitchell was assigned specifically to do instructor evaluations and a bit of management supervision. And despite his initial reservations about leaving his permanent duties for six weeks, he found he really enjoyed the evaluation work. Besides, he'd never worked with a more pleasant or professional group of people in the military.

Harvey was so busy with his new assignment that nearly four weeks passed before he had an opportunity to visit his colleagues in Fundamental Electronics. "When I walked in and headed for my office, I immediately noticed my name plate had been removed from the door," Harvey says. "When I got to my desk, I realized someone else had been working there."

> *"When I walked in and headed for my office, I immediately noticed my name plate had been removed from the door."*

Finding his personal possessions packed in a cardboard box in the corner of the office, Harvey went looking for Sergeant Sherman to ask for an explanation. "Well," the sergeant told him, "I've been discussing things with Major Zylinski and Colonel Webb. They were remembering how good you were in the F-16 program, and we agreed you could be a real asset in the F-15 program."

"Wait a minute!" responded Harvey. "I'm in Fundamentals now. No one has ever talked to me about the F-15 program!"

"Well, Harvey, we've just been talking about this, and it seemed the F-15 program really could use your leadership skills."

Harvey recognized a smoke screen when he saw it. "But why should I be reassigned?" he wanted to know. "Tell me the truth! What's going on here?"

"Okay," Sherman said, "to be perfectly honest with you, Harvey, what you told me about who you are and your personal beliefs—well, they kind of rub against my leadership style. They just aren't the way I work. And I perceived that in the future, you and I could run into some serious problems."

"But what problems are we having now?" Harvey asked.

His boss admitted, "I don't have a single problem with you now, Harvey. I respect you. I think you're a great guy and a first-rate instructor supervisor. Everything has been fine so far. But I have to tell you that I perceive that in the future, there will be a potential for problems because of our very different approaches and styles."

In more than 10 years with the military, Harvey had never heard of anyone being transferred because of a "perceived" problem that might occur in the future. Knowing such reasoning couldn't hold water, he went to see Major Zylinski, who had been his superior officer most of the time Harvey had been working as an instructor on that base. The major had recommended him for numerous performance awards, including "instructor of the year."

He confirmed what Sergeant Sherman had said. "There's no problem at all with your performance, Harvey," he explained. "It's just that Sergeant Sherman has told me he doesn't think you and he will work well together because of your different styles. So we are thinking everyone, including you, would be better served if you're in another capacity."

Harvey asked for an appointment to talk with Colonel Webb. "I'd known him almost as long as I'd known the major," Harvey says. "He was a Christian, so we'd had a number of personal conversations. Because he knew I was an assistant pastor of my church, one day he'd even asked me to pray with him in his office about a problem he was facing. So I felt I could be honest with him."

When Harvey told the colonel he didn't want a transfer, the colonel asked, "If you could have your pick of any job in the group, anywhere we could lateral you to, Harvey, what job would it be? Just tell me and the job is yours."

"How about Sergeant Sherman's?" Harvey asked.

"Impossible!"

"I know Fundamentals better than he ever will. I could do the job."

The colonel shook his head. "No, I don't think that would be possible," he insisted.

When Harvey made it clear he didn't want any transfer, the colonel deferred the decision back down to Major Zylinski. And while Harvey continued his temporary assignment with the StanEval team, his bosses began the paperwork for his transfer.

Harvey told his new colleagues what was going on. The entire StanEval team saw how upset he was. But they were also impressed with the way he was able to separate his emotions from the evaluation work he was doing so effectively. They tried to help by suggesting procedural ways to fight the transfer. With their encouragement, Harvey filed an official complaint saying Sergeant Sherman had discriminated against him because of personal bias with his feeling that "there could be a future problem."

Filing the complaint brought the transfer process to a grinding halt. And Colonel Webb called Harvey in for a conference. "I understand you filed a complaint," he said matter-of-factly.

"I did, sir," Harvey told him.

And then the colonel asked, as a personal favor, "Harvey, would you allow us to do the investigation internally?"

Because Harvey trusted the colonel, he said yes. And the colonel appointed another officer Harvey knew and trusted to conduct the investigation.

What Harvey didn't know was that Sergeant Sherman and Major Zylinski were so furious about the complaint that they called all the instructors together and "explained" that Harvey was evidently on some kind of power trip; that he wanted to be in charge of the school and end the Friday-afternoon beer parties Sergeant Sherman had instituted to improve morale; that he was so straitlaced he didn't want any of them to have any fun; and that he might personally keep the school from becoming the kind of elite program that would earn everyone recognition and awards.

"Then," Harvey explains, "when the investigator came in, the entire focus of the complaint was avoided. Instead of addressing my questioning of 'a perceived potential problem sometime in the future,' everyone treated the thing like a racial discrimination complaint. Because I'm black and Sergeant Sherman is white, that was the direction the investigator took with his questions: Do you think Sergeant Sherman is racially prejudiced? Have you seen any indication of Sergeant Sherman being racially discriminatory toward Sergeant Mitchell?"

Some of the people interviewed speculated that the real problems might be those "discussed" in the staff meeting—that Harvey Mitchell was perhaps "power hungry" and didn't want to get on board someone else's new program. Major Zylinski denied that he was prejudiced. He pointed to all the recommendations he'd made for the various awards Harvey had received under his command. "I've done nothing but help further Sergeant Mitchell's career," he told the investigator. "I have no idea why he's alleging bias. I'm disappointed that he's taken this route."

The inspector completed his job and concluded, "I find no evidence of discrimination against Sergeant Mitchell." The transfer could proceed.

When Harvey received his copy of the final report, he read it out loud to the guys in the StanEval office. When he finished, one of them commented, "That has nothing to do with your complaint." Another guy spoke up and said, "That's a snow job if I've ever heard one. They're sweeping the whole thing under the rug."

Everyone wanted Harvey to fight it. "You've gotta take this to the IG [inspector general]," they insisted. "Get someone from outside the organization to look at the real facts."

"You can beat this. They can't legally do what they're trying to do."

"You're in the right here, Harvey. Fight it. Take it to the next level. But you'd better do it soon, because your time with us is up in a little over a week."

With that advice from a team of top professionals whose job it was to know military procedure inside and out, Harvey went home that day prepared to do battle. He felt certain he would eventually win his fight. The only question in his mind was how high up he'd have to go before he'd be vindicated.

> *Just as sure as he knew he was in the right,*
> *Harvey realized that winning a fight like this might*
> *not be without serious professional cost.*

But just as sure as he knew he was in the right, Harvey realized that winning a fight like this might not be without serious professional cost. Even when you're right, if you fight the military system, you can be labeled as someone who's not a team player. So he called his parents to say, "You know, I've had a great military career. But I'm getting ready to do something that may jeopardize it." They assured him they'd stand behind him whatever he decided to do.

His wife, Carol, insisted, however, "You need to pray about this, honey. I know you're angry about the way you've been treated. But you need to be sure what God wants you to do."

The two of them began praying and counting the days until Harvey would finish his stint with StanEval and have to decide whether to accept his reassignment. Harvey told his church congregation the whole story and asked for their prayers as well.

"I went into this time of prayer looking for and expecting confirmation of my indignation," Harvey says. "After all, I was ultimately being persecuted for my Christian witness and beliefs. With the general staff and God on my side, I knew I'd be vindicated.

"I was hurt and confused about why some of the people I'd worked with could believe, let alone say, some of the things I read in that first inspector's report. But mostly I was angry and looking forward to vindication. However, as I prayed for the Lord's support and confirmation about fighting this battle, something strange happened. God began softening my heart by refocusing my attention from my enemies' unjust actions to their needs. Can you imagine how a man must be hurting spiritually to do something like Sergeant Sherman was doing to me?

"I remember thinking, *I don't want to imagine that. That's not where my pain is right now.* But as I continued to pray and search His Word, the Lord showed me verses like 'I'll fight your battles. I'll make your enemies my footstool.' I read that one over and over. I liked the idea of those guys getting turned into footstools. And I also read, 'No weapon formed against you shall prosper' and 'If God is for you, who can be against you?' And I thought, *Yeah! No way I'm gonna lose this thing.*"

But Harvey's ongoing effort to draw close to God and hear Him well only softened his heart further. "God began to turn the mirror of His Scripture toward me. He was saying, 'There's a lot of pride involved here. You've bought into all these honors you've won. You've bought into all the things men have said about you. Don't you see that when men lift you up, they can also let you down? But if you put Me first and let Me exalt you, then nobody can bring you down.'"

Harvey still wasn't ready to hear that. "Like Job, I wanted to argue with God, 'I'm in the right here. I haven't done anything wrong. It's those other guys who are wrong. Why is this happening to me?' And it was almost like the Lord was saying, 'Okay, Harvey, where were you when I made the heavens and the earth? How is it you know so much and are so self-righteous?'"

Harvey didn't want to hear that, either. But he did—loud and clear. And he admitted to Carol, "You know, honey, God is speaking to my heart. Maybe I've let some things go to my head. Maybe I'm standing here and wanting to fight more out of pride than anything else. Maybe I need to let go of my feelings and trust God to fight my battles for me.

"And my wife," says Harvey, "had the sweetest spirit. She simply said, 'Praise God!' She'd come to that conclusion on her own days before. But she'd just prayed and let God speak to me. And He did. God broke me. There on the potter's wheel were the broken pieces. And when my pride reached the point where I could allow God to add the moisture of humility, He was able to begin reshaping everything the way He wanted it."

Harvey told his church he'd decided not to pursue his complaint any further. The people there accepted that without any real questions. But when he told the StanEval team, they couldn't believe it. They told him:

"You can beat this, man. Everything is on your side."

"You've gotta fight 'em."

"You can't just go back in there now. They'll really be laying for you."

"It's got to come to this level at least. And you've already got this level won over."

But Harvey told them he'd made up his mind. He was returning to his unit and would do what was asked of him. "Going back there was one of the hardest things I've ever done," he says now. "Because when I went back to Fundamentals to pick up my personal items and say hello to some of my old friends, there were some instructors—long-time colleagues—who actually turned their backs and walked away rather than speak to me. That really grieved my heart."

When Harvey reported to the F-15 school, the person assigned to orient him was another old friend—Sergeant Sonny Henderson—who'd heard what had happened and told him, "I'm sorry it turned out this way."

"It's okay," Harvey told him. "I know you've got a job to do. So go ahead and give me the works."

Harvey's F-15 training began. During the course of that first morning, Sonny introduced him around to the other staff. It was clear from their reactions that they all knew, "This is the guy who lost his complaint." There was a wariness and an underlying suspicion that Harvey couldn't help but pick up on. It didn't exactly make him feel welcome.

During lunchtime, he got a call to report to Major Zylinski's office. The major, who was over several of the tech schools, had some questions about the annual performance reports Harvey had written up for each of the men he had supervised in Fundamentals. Each of the 10 reports had taken roughly half a day to complete, and he had done them on his own time while assigned to StanEval. The major said he'd read them and wanted to know why Harvey had not added "recommendations and endorsements," a report often attached to performance reviews to save the higher-ups time in the selection of awards and commendations.

Harvey replied, "Sir, according to regulations, I'm not required to do those. I did them as a favor in the past, but I had 10 of these reviews to do all at once, and if I wrote up recommendations and endorsements for each one, that would be 20 reports, and I've got all I can do to learn this new job you've put me in."

"Well," the major said, "you know it's common practice to do it, even if it's not in the regs."

"I understand that," Harvey told him. "But I'm not going to be able to do it at this time."

The major's eyes narrowed and his face reddened. "You're planning to play hardball on this, aren't you, Mitchell?" he said accusingly. "Well, I'm here to tell you that there's going to be a whole new ball game around here for you. And you'd better get used to it quick or you're going to have a tough time ahead of you in this outfit."

Harvey was so demoralized that he prayed every step of the way down the long flight of stairs from the major's office to the giant hangar floor. "Lord, You've gotta help me. I'm in big trouble."

As he walked along, it seemed as if Harvey's whole career flashed before his eyes. He explains, "I walked past an F-16—a marvel of electronic munitions yet as maneuverable as a cat in the sky. I'd spent years learning everything about that machine. I walked past an F-4, which we affectionately called 'The Pig' in Vietnam. I couldn't count the bruises I got working on that thing in the field because it's so low-slung and I'm six feet three and a half. I walked by an F-111, 'The Whispering Death,' it was called in Vietnam—an airplane so advanced you can push a button and it will follow the terrain to its target without the pilot ever touching the stick. I thought about how my career had started here and how proud I'd been to come back to tech school to teach other young men and women what I'd been taught so many years ago. And now it looked like my career might end right here as well. If my superiors were intent on doing me in, there wasn't much I could do to stop them."

All these things were racing through Harvey's mind as he walked from the hangar into the F-15 office and encountered a grinning Sonny Henderson. "Remember all that stuff I taught you this morning, buddy?" Sonny asked. "Well, you can forget it."

"What?" Harvey asked.

"You don't work here anymore!"

Harvey shook his head. "I just came from the major's office. Believe me, I work here."

"We just got a call. You're not going to work in F-15 or Fundamentals. You don't even work in the group anymore."

"What are you talking about, Sonny? Where am I going then?"

Sonny grinned wider. "You don't even work in this wing."

"Wow! You're kidding! Tell me what's going on."

"You work for the general, man. The folks at StanEval called to say you'd been selected to fill an opening on their permanent staff. You're to start processing out and report to headquarters immediately."

Harvey found the sudden change hard to believe. He called his friends at StanEval, and they confirmed everything. The commander of the team, Major Benjamin, had been so impressed with Harvey's performance and his ability to work effectively through his personal crisis that he'd wanted Harvey assigned to his team permanently. He'd passed the paperwork on to the vice-wing commander, the second in command beneath the general. Colonel Shaw sent a note back immediately saying, "I don't need to interview Harvey. I work with him on the base Chapel Fund Council every month. He'd make an excellent addition to your team. Hire him now!"

Just that quickly, on his very first day back in an unpleasant situation, Harvey was plucked out of reach of those who had opposed him and was reassigned to the most prestigious team on the entire base. Harvey could only thank God for hearing his prayer and delivering him.

Months passed. And every morning, Harvey continued to thank God for the way He'd fought the battle for him. Then one day he saw the schedule and felt his heart sink. "We're going to the 50th?" he asked. (That was his old unit.)

His friends on the StanEval team said, "Yeah, man, and if they've got dirty laundry to hide, they'd better hide it deep. Because we're going to find it!"

Harvey couldn't help thinking, *This is so amazing, Lord. I give this problem to You, I let You fight my battle, and You rescue me from the situation I'm in. And now, six months later, You stick a clipboard in my hand, put a pen in the other, give me the authority of a two-star general, and send me waltzing back in to judge the very outfit that treated me so badly. You're going to have to help me be fair here.*

(The rest of this story can be found in the Appendix, but we recommend you read it only after having your group discussion and completing the "My Response" section.)

Personal Evaluation

As you can see, their Christian faith was important to Jeff Vaughn and Harvey Mitchell as they made ethical decisions. How would you describe your relationship with Jesus Christ? Circle the letter of the answer that best reflects what you feel.

A. I'm in it for what I can get out of it.
B. I find myself angry at Him for not taking care of all my problems.
C. I am motivated to give since I've received so much.
D. I tend to be somewhat indifferent.

Think of a time when you (or someone you know) were accused of something you didn't do. What happened? How did it make you feel? How did you respond? What might you have done differently?

In the Group

1. What is an ethical dilemma you faced in the past? What did you do? What did you learn from the experience? Do you agree with the way Jeff Vaughn handled his situation? Why or why not?
2. Read through Hebrews 11 as a group. What does that chapter say about the perspective we need to keep in mind when choosing between pragmatism and a higher standard?
3. Would you have approached Sergeant Sherman, after his first profanity-filled speech, the same way Harvey Mitchell did? Why or why not? What might you have done differently?
4. Does letting the Lord fight our battles mean that we just kick back and get passive? When is letting go just a nice way to describe copping out? How do we know when we're trusting God?
5. Do hard work, dedication, and integrity guarantee success? Why or why not?
6. Given that Colonel Webb was a Christian, what assumptions did Harvey make about him? Were they accurate? What lesson should we learn from the colonel's part in the story?

My Response

Imagine yourself as Harvey at the end of the story. You're about to go back and evaluate the people who mistreated you. Now complete this sentence: If I were Harvey, I would handle the situation by _____

_____

_____

Memory Verse

"The LORD is my light and my salvation—whom shall I fear? The LORD is the stronghold of my life—of whom shall I be afraid?" (Ps. 27:1).

CHAPTER 2

Introduction

How is your relationship with your father? How about your relationship with your son (if you have one)? As the next story shows, it's all too possible for a father and son to go for years without really understanding each other or communicating very well. But as it also shows, it's never too late to take action and shape a better future.

Arnie Ruddinger had a lot to regret about the kind of dad he had been. Maybe you also have regrets, or perhaps your father does. All of us have made mistakes; none of us is perfect. That's where the grace of God comes in—as does our desire to make the future brighter no matter what the past has been like.

A Promise Keeper Believes It's Never Too Late to Start Over

rnie Ruddinger has devoted a lifetime to Christian service, working first in overseas missions and then with a parachurch ministry among college students. Likable and open-minded, Arnie has organizational and relational skills that have benefited countless young people over the years.

So it was with a sense of irony, regret, and guilt that he read a recent letter from his 40-year-old son, Jeremy, who wrote: "Dad, I've longed for most of my life to have a really close relationship with you. But so far it hasn't come about. It's important that I tell you this is a deeply felt need. And I'd like to see it happen."

Arnie's tears blurred the words on the page as he admitted, *I've really failed as a father.*

As painful as it was to read his son's words, the fact that Jeremy cared enough to express his longing for a better relationship raised a glimmer of hope in Arnie. He, too, felt that longing. And if they both wanted it, Arnie thought, *maybe it's not too late.* But when he asked himself, *So what am I going to do about it? How do we get from here to there?* he didn't have a clue.

This wasn't the first time Arnie Ruddinger sensed some of his shortcomings as a father. He remembers, "All three of our sons, as well as our daughter, always seemed to find it easier to talk to their mother than to me. Frances just seemed to have a gift I never had for drawing them out."

For years, Frances Ruddinger tried to encourage her husband's relationships with their children. "You know, dear," she'd say, "the boys really need your input." Or "I wish you would just give the children more attention."

Jeremy's letter brought back one particular memory of a time Arnie had been scanning the newspaper as Jeremy was trying to talk to him. Never lowering the pages to look at his son, he'd contented himself with a few distracted "Uh-huhs" as he continued to read. While it certainly wasn't the first or last time that happened, that particular incident stuck in his mind because of the way Frances had taken him to task later. "Didn't you realize what was going on, Arnie?" she said. "Couldn't you see Jeremy had something important he wanted to talk to you about? That he desperately wanted your feedback?"

Arnie says, "I remember telling her, 'No, I didn't notice. I guess I just wasn't aware of what was going on.' Like a lot of other times when Frances chided me about something in my relationship with the kids, I got a little defensive. Yet deep down, a part of me knew she had a greater sensitivity to our kids' needs than I did. Sometimes after Frances would say something about needing to show the children more attention, affection, or affirmation, I'd admit to myself (and once in a while even to her), *I know I need to do better in this area.* But I could never seem to change."

When they did talk honestly about it, Frances and Arnie could see an ingrained family pattern. Arnie's father had also found it difficult to connect with his children emotionally; Arnie had always felt a closer, warmer bond with his mother.

"After Frances and I would have one of these intense conversations about my fathering," Arnie says, "I'd usually feel guilty and do a lot of praying. I'd say, 'I feel like a failure, Lord. You've got to help me.'

"Looking back, knowing what I do now, I can't help thinking, *If I'd just had one other Christian man whom I could have sat down with and talked about my frustrations, who could have been a model for me, that might have made a tremendous difference.* But when I got to feeling guilty and inadequate, all I knew to do was go into my study and get with the Lord. I didn't have any other resource. And praying just didn't seem to do enough."

Not that the Ruddingers don't have a lot of wonderful family memories. Arnie recalls family trips and other special experiences with fondness, like the summer vacation to Lake Tahoe when the entire family hiked high into the mountains. "There were many good times like those when we all enjoyed not only the activities, but also the relationship we had as we did those things together," Arnie explains. "Yet it seems that on a day-to-day basis, there was always something lacking. I wasn't able to communicate that 'I'm really here for you; I'm truly interested and want to be involved in your lives.'"

Frances is quick to acknowledge Arnie's many positive attributes. For example, she says, "He has a great sense of humor and laughs a lot, which endears him to many people. He's a good and genuinely kind man." But she adds, "He had this lack of understanding about his family's emotional needs. And I think Jeremy and I probably felt that more than the other three children."

She goes on to say that for many years, she had to deal with her own anger over Arnie's lack of demonstrative attention to her and their marriage. When she suggested they go to a marriage counselor, Arnie was "surprised out of his socks." He'd had no more clue about what his wife needed and wanted that he did about his son.

Arnie had no more clue about what his wife needed and wanted than he did about his son.

One day, Frances says, when she was feeling particularly frustrated and sorry for herself, it was as if God clearly spoke to her. "You're making an idol of your marriage, Frances," He told her. "You want a perfect marriage, and you want your husband to love you in a perfect way. But Arnie can't do that. I'm the only One who can meet that need in your life."

Hearing that, Frances dropped to her knees beside the bed. With tears running down her cheeks, she promised God that from that day on, she would seek her need for a perfect, accepting, affirming love from Him alone. "God healed me right then and there," Frances says. "I was a different person. I never went back to that anger." And as she focused less on her own unmet needs, she felt she did a better job of responding to Arnie's. "As a result, our marriage has improved steadily since that point," Frances observes.

There was no parallel improvement in the relationship between Arnie and their children, however. Jeremy especially looks back on his growing-up years and remembers his father frequently being away from home on business. "It wasn't so much his being gone physically that bothered me," Jeremy says. "It was that he was gone even more emotionally. When he *was* home, we seldom seemed to connect on a meaningful level."

In time, Frances came to better understand her husband's emotional distance from his family. Not only were many of his personality traits and behavioral patterns much like his own father's, but there had also been a period during Arnie's childhood when he'd been separated from his parents. "Arnie apparently buried his hurt in his heart and managed to always be a good little boy who could deny his painful emotions," Frances says. "But he became a colder, less emotionally oriented person as a result."

"I don't remember ever being angry about that lack of closeness," Jeremy says. "I just came to accept it as the way things were going to be between us. But acceptance didn't prevent a sense of loss and sadness and pain."

All three Ruddingers agree that for whatever reason, Jeremy was probably the one child Arnie had the most difficult time relating to. Frances says she sees many similarities (in terms of personality, motivation, and interests) between Arnie and Jeremy. That could be one factor complicating their relationship.

Arnie acknowledges, "Jeremy has always seemed a little different from the other boys, like he wasn't cut out of the same cloth. He's chosen his own course. And I think he has sensed that I've found it hard to affirm, accept, or even understand some of his choices."

Jeremy adds, "My guess is that he's seen me as the child he feels most distant from because I've probably been the least traditional of his sons. Even my older brother, who started out the prodigal, ended up in a more traditional position as a successful medical doctor. Mine has been much more of a winding career path."

The conflict over Jeremy's career choices first surfaced during his college years, as he struggled with what to major in and sought God's direction for his life's work. He and his father exchanged numerous letters during those years. Jeremy would write of his uncertainty, and Arnie would respond with a long list of suggestions. As Jeremy remembers, "One of my father's primary gifts has always been organization and planning. So he'd send me all these carefully-thought-out and logical suggestions about what steps I could take to do this or that. But those letters were always painful reminders that he didn't know me well enough to realize few of those suggestions fit me at all. Since they weren't helpful, I didn't follow them, and that increased the awkwardness between us."

When Jeremy graduated from college, Arnie's ongoing concern that he find and pursue some clear direction intensified the lack of acceptance and affirmation Jeremy felt. Then Jeremy was befriended and mentored for a time by an older Christian named John. This man encouraged Jeremy to find his identity in his relationship with God before worrying about what career path to follow. No one had ever affected Jeremy's thinking like John. And in talking to Arnie about this mentoring relationship, Jeremy says, "I probably hurt my father by indicating, if not in actual words, then certainly by my attitude, that 'Here's someone who knows me better than you do. His affirmation and acceptance have helped me more than you have.'"

Arnie also had initial reservations about Jeremy's girlfriend, Marsha, in the early days of their courtship. (She later became his wife.) "I just wasn't convinced she was right for Jeremy," Arnie says. He adds that he has changed his mind about that now and regularly thanks God for Marsha's presence in Jeremy's life. But his son and daughter-in-law haven't always felt that acceptance.

Arnie had trouble, too, with Jeremy's and Marsha's decision to pursue a simple—what Arnie terms a countercultural—lifestyle. They've had seven children, all but one born at home with the help of a midwife. They home-school, raise much of their own food on the land around their small country home, and are strict conservationists.

But the single biggest factor making Jeremy seem different in Arnie's eyes is that his son has been content to work at a long string of relatively low-paying, blue-collar jobs. For the last several years, Jeremy has worked for a man in the house-painting business. While Arnie always tried to couch his concern in economic terms, worrying how his son would provide for the needs of his growing family, Jeremy couldn't help sensing that familiar feeling—that his father still didn't accept him for the person he is.

> *Jeremy couldn't help sensing that familiar feeling—that his father still didn't accept him for the person he is.*

Over time, Jeremy's wife helped him recognize how his relationship with his father was affecting his own role as a man and dad. "I never remember consciously missing out on physical affection from my father as I was growing up," Jeremy says. "But I'm grateful to have a wife like Marsha who encourages me to be physically affectionate with her and our children. I enjoy giving it. But I have to work at it deliberately. It doesn't come naturally."

Jeremy says Marsha has provided him with other insights as well: "She reminds me to look my father in the eye when we talk, because she noticed I don't make good eye contact with him. We've tried to analyze that, and my conclusion is that it was a defense mechanism I developed over the years. Sort of *If he doesn't give me enough attention, I won't give him* my *full attention*. When I realized what was going on, it saddened me and made me want to really work on our relationship."

All of this is background for understanding the impact of that letter Jeremy wrote his dad during the winter of 1993, when he expressed his desire for a closer, more meaningful relationship. It also helps explain why, though his son's letter moved Arnie to tears and stirred in him a renewed longing for the same kind of relationship, he still didn't know what to do about it.

During that same period, Arnie first heard of Promise Keepers. Much of what he learned interested him. And after listening to a couple of Focus on the Family radio programs highlighting the ministry, he signed up to attend the 1993 conference in Boulder. That weekend, according to Arnie, was a pivotal experience. "I don't remember any one speaker or message," he says. "It was the overall impact that ministered to me. Here were all these Christian men gathered together, who despite their past failures and because of them were determined to become better Promise Keepers.

"God spoke very clearly to me there. He expanded my understanding of the role of a father, a husband, and a man of God. He convinced me of the need to deal with my family life, particularly my relationship with Jeremy, in a more intentional way. I saw that He wanted me to commit this area of my life to Him and allow Him to work in me and on me."

One of the first things Arnie did when he got home was to write his sons a long letter describing what had happened to him at the conference. He told how God had been speaking to him about improving his relationships with them, and he asked all three boys to join him at the Promise Keepers conference in Indianapolis the following year.

They agreed to go. And the four Ruddinger men traveled together to Indiana in June 1994. For Arnie, it was a meaningful experience. The drive home, during which they each said how God had spoken to them, was especially memorable. "That was perhaps the most significant time for us together as the men of the family," he says. "I sensed a new openness between us."

Jeremy admits that for him, however, the weekend was a little disappointing. After all his father had said about the conference the year before, he'd hoped for more of a breakthrough experience—perhaps a sudden and radical transformation in their relationship. Instead, he's learning that life-long patterns usually take time to change.

Yet all the Ruddingers acknowledge that change is, indeed, taking place. Arnie says, "I sense a new freedom to open up with each other. I think we've still got a long way to go—I know I do—but I want to build on this and see it continue." He cites the most recent family Thanksgiving gathering, where all his sons and their wives described how the Lord had worked in their lives over the preceding year. "Tears were shed that day," Arnie says. "And afterward, when all our children had gone home, Frances and I praised God with deep emotion for the new spirit of honesty and openness we'd felt."

According to Arnie, the Lord is also helping change some of his attitudes toward Jeremy. "I've reached a point of genuine appreciation for Jeremy that I've never felt before," he says. "I've even gained a peace about where he's at in his career. I wish he was in a more stable financial situation, but I recognize such godly qualities developing in him and his wife and their children that I have to step back and say, 'Thank You,

Lord, for what You're doing in Jeremy's life. You're raising up a man who is seeking after You.'

"He and Marsha are wonderful parents, and all their children are developing so well. Seeing that, I've come to not only appreciate Jeremy, but to truly respect him for the person he is. It's taken me a long time to reach this point. And it's only a combination of God's grace, the years of admonitions of my loving wife, and the insights gained through Promise Keepers that has brought me here."

Arnie is still in the process of conveying this change of attitude convincingly to his son. Jeremy agrees their relationship still has a long way to go. But he's quick to add that he has renewed respect and appreciation for his father. "The fact that we both have now voiced the need to improve our relationship is an important step," Jeremy says. "While I think he still struggles to know how to do it, I admire his willingness to admit his need for change and his deficiencies in relating to me. I realize a lot of fathers would never have been able to do that. It's just that progress hasn't come as quickly or as easily as I would wish."

Yet Arnie and Jeremy both share Frances Ruddinger's sense of hopefulness about their relationship. "I'm deeply grateful," she says, drawing on Joel 2:25, "that the Lord is now restoring the years the locusts have eaten."

Personal Evaluation

On a scale from 1 (not good at all) to 10 (excellent), how would you rate your relationship with your father? (If he has already passed away, how would you have rated it at the time of his death?) Why?

If you're a father yourself, using the same scale, how would you rate the most difficult relationship you have with one of your children? Why? What one thing could you do to move it closer to a 10?

In the Group

1. How did you fill in the blank at the end of the last session about evaluating your old unit in the place of Harvey Mitchell? Why did you choose that response?

2. Did you relate more to Arnie or Jeremy in this story? Why?

3. What are some of the hopeful signs that Arnie and Jeremy's relationship is getting stronger?

4. Which of your traits or dreams did your father have a hard time understanding? Why? Which of your children's traits or dreams do you have a hard time with? Why?

5. No doubt Arnie had tried to be the best father he knew how to be. How do you suppose he had been reared by his own dad? How have expectations of fathers changed in the past 40 years?

6. Arnie indicated that having a Christian man to talk with about his parental expectations and frustrations would have been a big help. This is in keeping with Proverbs 27:17, which says, "As iron sharpens iron, so one man sharpens another." Who is that man you can talk to? If you don't have such a helper, whom might you recruit?

7. If a man's father or child is still alive and their relationship isn't what one or both of them would like it to be, what first step(s) could they take to work things out?

My Response

Like Jeremy, you might want to write a letter expressing your feelings to your father (or your child, if that's your need). What things would you need to say in that letter? (It will help you to write it even if your father is deceased.

And if your relationship is very good, you can write words of praise and thanks.)

_____

_____

Plan a time in the next couple of weeks to write and send (if possible) that letter.

Memory Verse
"He will turn the hearts of the fathers to their children, and the hearts of the children to their fathers" (Mal. 4:6).

CHAPTER 3

Introduction

What would you do if a long-dreamed-of goal suddenly seemed to conflict with your commitment to be a Promise Keeper with your family? That's the situation in which Sam Wainwright found himself, and he soon faced some painful choices.

Going ahead with his dream would mean sacrifices for a long season for Sam and his wife. As you read his story, think about the decisions he had to make, the options that might have been available to him, and the way he went about trying to discern God's will.

A Promise Keeper Seeks to Know God's Will

L ike a lot of guys, when Sam Wainwright got out of high school and reached the edge of adulthood without a clear objective, he joined the service. The Army trained him in the field of electronic communications, and it also took a northeasterner and introduced him to life in the Deep South. While there, he met and married a woman with a young daughter.

"I hadn't been raised in a Christian home, but my parents had a stable, committed marriage," Sam says. "So even though I had little understanding of what marriage was or should be, I went into it thinking 'for life.'" His wife seemed to have no such ideals. Sam wasn't her first choice in men and clearly wouldn't be her last. When things were going well in their relationship, she seemed happy enough; when they weren't, she figured, *There are other guys around.* And there always were.

"But the truth is," Sam admits, "neither of us knew what it took to make a marriage relationship work."

Meanwhile, Sam learned an important lesson in the Army. He enjoyed his experience in electronics, but his time in the field taught him, as he says, "that I really preferred working with people rather than things. Helping people seemed so much more satisfying than fixing and maintaining machines." So when he left the service, he took a tour of a local hospital and decided to become a medical technician. He worked for a time in the hospital lab and then did on-the-job training as a respiratory therapist.

"I found a level of fulfillment I'd never known before," Sam recalls. "There were times I worked 16-hour shifts without feeling the least bit tired. I quickly decided, *It's the medical field for me. This is great!* And who's at the top in medicine? Doctors, of course. So I decided I'd become a doctor."

This was no casual decision on Sam's part. He immediately began full-time work on a college degree while continuing his career as a respiratory therapist. But his marriage ended before he completed his undergraduate studies, and he came out of college feeling emotionally unprepared to consider med school.

Though he put his plans on hold for a couple of years, Sam never lost sight of his dream. He continued to take additional college courses to broaden his background and improve his chances of getting into med school when he did apply. He went so far as to ask a member of the admissions committee of the school he wanted to attend for her recommendations on what further steps would enhance his record. And Sam followed the woman's advice, some terms taking a full load of classes in subjects she suggested.

During this period, Sam accepted an invitation to join a church missions team for a one-week trip to Peru. Also on the team were a doctor friend, Fred Stevens, and a local pastor. "I felt rather proud to realize my professional services could be used in such a way for God," Sam says. "But it didn't take me long to realize God wanted me on that trip not to make use of my medical skills but to show me the depth of my own spiritual needs."

From the start of the trip, Dr. Stevens and the pastor talked about the Lord in such a personal way that Sam felt uncomfortable. And when the Peruvian Christians, who were so vocal about their faith in the face of adverse circumstances, questioned Sam about his Christian commitment, he realized he didn't have much to say to them. Their spiritual examples convicted him even more than they inspired him. While attending a baptismal service there in Peru with the other members of his team, Sam realized he'd never trusted in Jesus as his own personal Savior. He made that decision and was baptized during the same service.

Another memorable experience for Sam took place during that trip. He explains: "As a respiratory therapist, I had purchased the best stethoscope money could buy with plans to grow into it someday after I made it through med school. It was a concrete, daily reminder of my dream. I'd even had it engraved.

"I had taken it to Peru and had it with me one day when Fred Stevens and I were attending a patient with a young Peruvian doctor. This doctor had only the cheapest of stethoscopes—something a nursing student might pick up for five or ten dollars here in the States. Seeing her listening intently to her patient's chest with her inferior stethoscope, Fred reached over, took mine, and handed it to her while saying through our interpreter, 'Here. Take this.'

"When the doctor looked up in surprise, Fred smiled and told her, 'I have many stethoscopes. You keep this.'

"At that point my jaw dropped, and I felt the color drain out of my face. Obviously the young doctor noticed, because she got this puzzled look on her face as Fred tried to tell me, 'Don't worry about it.'

"When she asked, 'What's the matter?' Fred explained that it was actually my stethoscope. So she asked me, 'Do you have many stethoscopes as well?'

"'No,' I admitted, 'but I want you to have it.' That wasn't exactly true at the moment I said it, but the look of joy on her face was worth the price of that stethoscope." (Dr. Stevens later replaced Sam's stethoscope.)

So Sam returned from that missions trip spiritually humbled and renewed. He was also ready to begin looking toward the future again—personally as well as professionally. He started dating a committed Christian woman he'd first met through his church. Susan, too, had been healing from the emotional aftermath of a divorce from a spouse who had never shared her faith. They were both cautiously seeking someone who saw a serious Christian commitment as an essential part of any relationship. They hit it off from the start.

Susan, who had exposure to the medical field in her job as a pediatric physical therapist, understood and affirmed Sam's continuing dream of attending medical school. With her encouragement, Sam decided he was finally ready to take his med school admissions test (MCAT) and formally apply to the state university's medical center.

The return letter from the application committee came late in the spring of 1990. He had been accepted as an alternate, which meant that all the positions had been filled, but that if anyone who'd been officially accepted changed his or her mind or didn't follow through, Sam was on a list of those who would be considered to fill the slot.

Sam's reaction reflected his optimistic nature. "I never actually knew whether there were three alternates or 10 or even 50," he says. "But at the time I thought, *I almost made it! I'm that close to my goal. What more can I do to make sure I get accepted next year?"*

He kept working, signed up for more preparatory college courses, and took the MCAT again the next spring. This time when the letter arrived from the med school, Sam didn't open it right away. Susan, who by now had accepted his proposal of marriage and was anticipating a wedding just weeks away, says, "He wanted to pray about it for a few days, asking the Lord to prepare him to accept whatever the decision was. I appreciated that attitude of submission, but the suspense almost drove me insane, because I knew how much his dream meant to him."

Sam vividly recalls opening the letter and reading that his application had been turned down.

Sam vividly recalls opening the letter and reading that his application had been turned down. "It was a devastating rejection. The worst I'd expected was to be an alternate again. If anything, my application was *stronger* than the year before. It was the one thing I wasn't prepared for. But there was no telling myself, *You almost made it.* There was nothing to be encouraged about."

Susan and he wept together as she shared his pain. And Sam prayed, "What's going on here, Lord? What are You trying to tell me?"

At that point he felt the Lord was asking him, "How much is this worth to you?" And he told Him, "I'll do whatever it takes!"

Susan could see how hurt Sam was. But she admired his response: "If anything, the rejection seemed to make him even more determined. He set right out to do whatever he could to better impress the committee the next year."

Sam and Susan married and began their new life together. And everything they planned for their future included Sam's goal of becoming a doctor. Susan was as impressed by her husband's motives as she was by his determination. When they talked about the day he would be a physician, his focus was never on the prestige or money a medical degree might bring. Sam instead imagined how he might serve others as a doctor—maybe opening a clinic in some rural Southern county that had no medical care. He remained totally open to whatever specialty the Lord might direct him toward. Sam's motives seemed so pure that Susan couldn't imagine why God hadn't thrown the doors wide open for him.

What had happened was that the medical school had the strongest pool of applicants it had seen in years. There were so many top-notch applicants that Sam simply didn't make the cut that year. Yet he kept studying and plugging away through that first year of marriage to Susan. And the next spring, he took the tests and applied for the third time.

"When I made the alternate list once again, I wasn't very disappointed," Sam says. "I felt it was a step in the right direction." The following year he took a special study course and met a number of Christian pre-med students. They scheduled a prayer breakfast just before taking the MCAT, and Sam came out of that day-long test for the first time feeling very good about it. Indeed, he posted his best score to date. So he felt more confident than ever about his application.

When the letter with the telltale return address finally arrived, Sam took the stack of mail home and waited for Susan. That night when they were together, they prayed and opened the envelope. "Susan and I cried together again—this time for joy," Sam remembers. "I was in. After all those years and all that effort, I was finally *in*. My dream was going to come true."

"It was wonderful," Susan adds. "Sam was so high! I took pictures of him reading the letter. He called his parents to tell them the news. Then we celebrated by going out to eat at our favorite restaurant."

However, that was a sobering time for the Wainwrights as well, because the prospect of Sam starting med school that fall forced them to consider the difficult years ahead. "The thought of me being the sole financial support while Sam was in school seemed a little scary," admits Susan. "But mostly it was a time of happy excitement and anticipation, because Sam had worked so hard and dreamed about this day for so long."

During that same spring, Sam first heard about Promise Keepers on Focus on the Family's radio show. "Everything they said about Promise Keepers made me think, *That sounds like something I really need*," he says. "Their emphasis on placing God first and the sacredness of marriage and family seemed like the foundation I would need to help get me through the demands of med school. From that first time I heard about the conference, I felt almost compelled to go. It was a 'now or never' kind of feeling, because I knew what lay ahead."

Sam set out to recruit a group of men to go to Boulder with him. Several agreed; all but one eventually backed out. And when the two of them got to

Colorado, that guy, an anthropology student, heard his own personal call of the wild and headed on to Wyoming to study Indians. Sam went to the conference by himself.

"So much of what I heard those two days hit home," Sam says. "But the real kicker came at the end of the conference, in a special closing candlelight service, when Bill McCartney laid out the challenge and called for men who would be true Promise Keepers. My first reaction was *I can't be a Promise Keeper. I'm just not going to have the time to make this commitment.* But then I realized that if I wasn't going to be able to put God and my family first in my life, something was very wrong. This was a shocking thought because of the implications for my dream. Could it possibly be that God did *not* want me to become a doctor? I sat there wrestling with those issues, but I didn't have long to think if I was going to participate in the ceremony. I couldn't sort everything out in so short a time, but there was no doubt that God and my family should come before any vocation. So I accepted and lit my candle as a symbol of my commitment."

> *"I realized that if I wasn't going to be able to put*
> *God and my family first in my life,*
> *something was very wrong."*

Sam went home from Colorado, and with tears in his eyes he told Susan, "Part of me can't believe I'm saying this, but I've made a commitment to put God and our marriage ahead of everything else in my life. And if I can't keep those commitments while going to med school, I'm prepared to give up my dream of becoming a doctor."

His wife says, "It made me sad to think Sam might face that decision after all he went through to get accepted into med school. But I was proud of the commitment he was making to the Lord and to our relationship."

School started that fall. "On the one hand, it was a long-awaited, deeply desired, God-given dream come true," Sam says. "Everything I'd wanted for so long was finally falling into place. I had a wonderful marriage, a godly wife, I was in med school, and I was going to be a physician. The course work was challenging, and the pressure was frustrating. But at the same time, I found the experience exciting and rewarding. I loved the work."

It became obvious in the first few days, however, that the demands and the schedule were going to make school all consuming. Sam would get up by five every morning to pray as quickly as possible before hitting the books. He'd arrive at school before seven and spend the time before his first class in the anatomy lab, reviewing the previous day's dissection. From nine until five or six in the evening, he would be in class. Then he'd hurry home, eat a quick supper, and study until midnight before collapsing into bed. He was determined to take one evening off a week to spend with Susan, but that never seemed enough time.

"I loved what I was doing," he says. "But I felt as if I was losing more of what really meant the most to me. My walk with the Lord, my marriage, and plans for a family all seemed to be on hold. And there were four long years of school ahead of me and another four years of residency."

During this time, Sam began to get calls from other men in the area who'd been to Promise Keepers or were interested in the ministry. Some just wanted information, but others hoped to get a local men's group started. To each person who phoned, Sam said, "I really believe in what this organization is trying to do. It's wonderful. It's been very meaningful to me. But I just don't have time to get involved right now."

Each time he had to say that, he felt as if he were denying Christ. And that began to weigh heavily on his mind. "I felt I was putting the wrong things first—that medicine was taking me away from where I knew I needed to be," he says. "It was an agonizing struggle."

Fred Stevens, the Christian physician friend who'd gone to Peru with Sam, was a big help during this time. Sam dropped by his office frequently to pray with him, and Fred encouraged him to be sensitive to what God was telling him. That wasn't easy for Sam to hear. But as the weeks passed, one question Fred asked really crystallized the issue for Sam: "Do you feel you're closer to the Lord and to Susan now than before you started school?"

"The answer to that was so obviously *No!*" Sam says.

Yet how could he give up on his dream? Sam talked with his contact on the admissions committee. She was a Christian herself and sympathetic to his struggle. Years before, because of her own family priorities, she had pursued a Ph.D. instead of going into med school.

Most of the counsel Sam received from the medical community was that he should stick it out. One physician, a neurosurgeon he'd known for years, stopped him in the hall at the medical center one day to let him know he'd heard about Sam's doubts. He said that in his opinion, it should be illegal for any first-year medical student to drop out of school. "Everyone hates it the first year," he said.

"That just wasn't true in my case," Sam says. "I didn't hate med school at all. I enjoyed the work. So it wasn't a matter of hating it and wanting out. My question was, 'Is this really best for my family and for me spiritually?' I could try to rationalize staying by thinking about how much better my family's future financial picture would be as a physician. I could imagine how much I could do for the Lord as a medical missionary. But such thoughts felt more and more like rationalizations."

Susan witnessed her husband's struggle up close. "From the day he started med school, Sam wasn't himself. I could tell just by looking at him—there was no peace about him. When we had time together, which wasn't much, Sam talked about his dilemma. And I began to feel that if med school was really something God wanted him to do, he wouldn't be in such torment over it. But I hesitated to say that, because I didn't want anything I said to be the trigger that ended his dream. That was something Sam would have to see and decide for himself. So I just prayed and turned him over to the Lord."

One day near the end of his first month in med school, Sam realized his inner struggle was no longer over what he should do, it was over not doing it. That morning before he left for school, he told Susan he'd made up his mind.

(To help you imagine yourself in Sam's place and think through the issues he faced, we have chosen not to reveal what Sam decided to do.)

Personal Evaluation

If your wife or children were asked how you spend your time, would you mind having their answers printed in the newspaper for everyone to see? Why or why not?

In the Group

1. Did you write the letter discussed in the "My Response" section of the preceding session? If so, did you deliver it? If you didn't write it or you wrote it but didn't send it, why did you make that decision?

2. What does your daily use of time reveal about your true priorities? Are those priorities what you want them to be? Why or why not?

3. What have you personally given up to enrich your family? What have you received from your investment?

4. How do we determine God's will for our lives, including our careers? What biblical passages support the methods you suggest?

5. Priorities aren't set in stone; they're dynamic. In Sam's case, he and his wife had agreed that for a time, he would need to concentrate on his medical studies and give less time to other things. Why do you think Sam's perspective changed? How might he and his wife have worked more closely together in making a decision (e.g., by jointly making a pros-and-cons list for each option and studying relevant Scriptures)?

6. What biblical passages might apply to Sam's situation? to your own priority setting?

7. Optional: If someone in your group is facing a big decision right now, help him by talking through a pros-and-cons list for each of his options and identifying passages of Scripture that might apply.

My Response

Complete this prayer in keeping with your unique situation, and then say it to God: "Lord, my biggest struggle in keeping my priorities straight right now is _____

Help me to know and do Your will in this area. Thank You for loving me and hearing my prayer, in Jesus' name. Amen."

Memory Verse

" 'For I know the plans I have for you,' declares the LORD, 'plans to prosper you and not to harm you, plans to give you hope and a future' "(Jer. 29:11).

CHAPTER 4

Introduction

Like many of us, Joel Treadaway wrestled with his priorities. Balancing the demands of marriage, children, and career was a constant challenge.

We suspect many readers will identify with that struggle. You may, in fact, find parts of Joel's story uncomfortably similar to your own. But as you read, think through his choices and what you can learn from them, and then apply those lessons to your own situation.

A Promise Keeper Strengthens
His Marriage

Joel and Lena Treadaway's marriage didn't get off to an easy start by anyone's standards. The wedding took place a week before Joel started law school. Lena was also in college, finishing up her work for a teaching degree. "So we didn't actually experience our first year of marriage until after Joel graduated from law school," Lena says. "He was so committed to his studies that I hardly saw him before then."

And at that point, Lena's workaholic husband merely traded one obsession for another. Instead of school, he now threw all his energies into his fledgling career at a large Miami firm. He not only worked hard, but he was good, too. In less than three years, Joel became the youngest partner in the history of the 200-lawyer firm.

He achieved that success, however, at the expense of a healthy marriage. Learning they would be unable to have children, something they both wanted, only added to the strain. So by the time they began discussing the implications of adoption, Lena knew something had to change.

Joel kept telling her, "When I catch up on my work, we'll have some time to spend together." They even scheduled a couple of vacation trips, only to have Joel cancel their plans at the last minute each time.

Lena finally demanded to go along one day when Joel had to drive to north Florida for a deposition. At least that would give them a chance to talk. As they drove, she poured out her frustration and unhappiness. "We've got to do something, because this just isn't going to work," she told him. "We're thinking about adoption, but I don't think it would be fair to bring a child into our home right now. You're totally involved in your career. You're never home. We don't talk. We never do things together. This is not the kind of life I want."

By evening, there seemed nothing left to say. "So there in some stinky-dinky motel somewhere in north Florida," Lena recalls, "I told him, 'I can't go on living like this. We're already living separate lives; why not make it official? Divide up our things and begin divorce proceedings.'"

> ### "We're already living separate lives; why not make it official? Divide up our things and begin divorce proceedings."

Joel turned and looked into his wife's eyes. In a halting, tortured voice, he asked, "Lena, is that really what you want?"

Lena bowed her head and closed her eyes tight in an attempt to hold in the tears. Silently she prayed, "God, if You're real, I'm going to ask You to take away my anger." She says, "God absolutely, instantaneously melted my heart. I slowly raised my head and said, 'We'll try it again.' And as I looked deep into Joel's brown eyes, I sensed an intensity and a depth of love between us that we'd never had before."

Joel felt it, too. "I realized we'd reached a crisis point," he says. "I had to come to grips with some crucial questions. Was I going to be a real husband and father? Or was I going to go off by myself in pursuit of a career?

"We were both Christians at the time. But there was a lot more to marriage than going to church together, paying the bills, and fixing up the house together." Joel had been going through those motions and neglecting a lot of other things. So he made a commitment to Lena and to God that he was going to straighten out his priorities.

Joel figured, *If I can organize my professional life enough to succeed as a trial lawyer, I ought to be able to organize my entire life in a way that I can also be a successful husband and father!*

For starters, Joel told Lena, "From now on, when I schedule vacation time, we'll do it. I won't let anything interfere." They spent several good blocks of time together over the following months. But that wasn't all. Joel made a point of taking Lena on a date at least once a week—to eat out or maybe to a movie. Knowing his wife had grown up a country girl who hadn't been excited about living in a big city, he arranged a garden plot for Lena on land one of his senior partners owned outside of town. Almost every weekend, the two of them would drive out to tend their garden.

"Not that everything was suddenly perfect," Lena says. "Joel still worked very hard. Whenever he took time off, he'd go back and work extra-long hours to make up for it. He was still very conscientious, almost obsessive at times, about his work responsibilities. But it was like he was a different man. When he *was* home, he was *home*. He showed an interest in what I was doing and who I was. He was committed to me as a person. I knew he cared about me. That's what I noticed more than anything else: He really cared."

The Treadaways' new commitment to each other and their marriage provided a much-needed foundation for the often-challenging experience of parenthood. They adopted a little boy they named Danny. A couple of years later, to their astonishment, Lena became pregnant with a little boy they named Isaac; sadly, he was stillborn. When Danny was three and a half, they adopted Sara. At her six months checkup, doctors discovered an extremely serious birth defect requiring delicate and dangerous open-heart surgery.

"Those were stressful, difficult years," Lena admits. "But Joel was so good, so sensitive in every crisis. He was with me 100 percent of the time in the hospital with Isaac. And he was there with me the entire time of Sara's surgery. I doubt I could have survived any of that without Joel's consistent and loving support."

The Treadaways never imagined their toughest ordeal was yet to come. It began when the adoption agency that had placed Danny and Sara called to tell them about an unwanted newborn boy with a terminal heart problem in a nearby hospital. The baby had suffered one massive heart attack right after birth. The next would almost certainly kill him. Doctors expected him to die at any moment. But in the meantime, the agency was looking for a couple who knew something about neonatal heart problems and would be willing to visit and hold and comfort the little boy.

One visit to the hospital nursery was enough to convince both Joel and Lena that they wanted to adopt Seth. Within three weeks, the little guy amazed the doctors by growing strong enough for the Treadaways to take him home. But two days later, his heart stopped, and he had to be resuscitated and rushed back into the hospital. The doctors gave him six months to live—maximum.

Countless people prayed for Seth. As he grew bigger and stronger, his astonished doctors considered him a miracle boy. His heart stopped on several occasions, but each time the Treadaways or some medical personnel were able to revive him. He was in and out of the hospital for months. And when he was home, he required 24-hour-a-day attention.

Because Joel had to work, most of the strain of Seth's daily care fell on Lena. But Joel made a special effort to shoulder the bulk of the load on weekends and even made most of the doctor's appointments during the week.

Joel bonded with Seth in a way that amazed Lena and gave her a new depth of love and admiration for her husband. But Joel's devotion to Seth also gave her reason to worry: The longer their son defied medical odds, the more Joel wanted to believe that Seth might actually be able to live a normal life someday.

By the time Seth turned two, his general health had improved to the point that he could get out of the house and go places with the family. Though short on physical stamina and speed, and still requiring regular medication and at least daily respiratory therapy, he was very much an active boy. While Lena concurred with Joel in feeling they needed to start treating Seth as normally as possible, she worried more and more about what she considered Joel's Pollyanna attitude. Her own joy over Seth's remarkable survival and growth was always tempered by the realization that his heart problem remained and could kill him at any time.

Even so, Lena and the rest of the family thrilled at the remarkable results of what Joel termed their "Challenge Seth Program." Though he didn't have the upper body strength to actually swim, Seth dearly enjoyed floating and kicking in the water. Horseback riding became a special joy for him. But what he may have loved best of all was skiing, with Joel holding him upright between his legs as they descended the slopes.

Joel was so heartened by all Seth could do that he became reluctant to talk about his son's continuing medical problems. About the time Seth turned four and Lena began to sense a subtle but steady decline in his overall strength, Joel couldn't (or wouldn't) see it. But then maybe he subconsciously saw what was coming, because he began to withdraw from the family by becoming more and more wrapped up in his work.

One night during the summer of 1992, as Lena was putting Seth down for the night, she asked him, "Do you know how much I love you?"

He gave her a big hug and said, "Oooh, I love you, too."

At that point, Lena says she felt something prod her to continue: "Do you know Jesus loves you that much, too?"

"Yeah, I know," he replied. "Mommy . . . Jesus is here."

"He certainly is, honey," Lena assured him. Then she noticed that instead of looking at her, Seth was staring across the room toward his bookshelf.

Then he pointed and said, "He's right over there."

"Is He?" she asked.

"Yes."

Lena followed her son's gaze. "I never saw anything," she says. "But I had no doubt Seth could. For what seemed like five minutes, I sat in silence, watching him stare toward that bookcase. Then he got this real sweet smile on his face and finally looked back to me. I told him, 'Seth, if Jesus ever wants you to go with Him, I want you to go. It's okay. Because He loves you that much.'

"He said, 'Okay, Mommy, I will,' and then he looked back over toward the bookcase and smiled real, real big. I got up to leave. And when I had walked out into the hall, I just collapsed against the wall, because I knew the end was coming."

Joel was home that night. But Lena didn't tell him what had happened because she didn't think he wanted to hear it. He certainly didn't want to acknowledge what became even more obvious to Lena over the next four weeks: Seth was growing weaker and weaker.

Then, one afternoon while sitting peacefully in Lena's lap, Seth stopped breathing. As she laid him quickly on his bed and began administering CPR, she yelled for Danny to call 911 and then Joel's office. But she knew her son was gone.

The paramedics had arrived and taken over the CPR by the time Joel called on his car phone to say he was on his way. "What happened?" he wanted to know.

"Seth just died," Lena told him.

"What do you mean, *died?*"

Lena gently replied, "Honey, he's gone. We can't bring him back this time. This is it!"

"Why do you say that?" he demanded.

"Because it's true. There's just this peace. It's over."

Then Joel said, "I'll be right there."

"Okay. You want to talk some more?" Lena asked.

"No, I want to be alone."

Joel actually met Lena at the hospital, where she says her husband "absolutely fell apart. He'd been in denial for so long that he had to cry."

The Treadaways planned a special funeral they called a celebration service. After people described some of their favorite memories of Seth, the family launched helium balloons into the sky to symbolize their release of their son to God in heaven.

But despite their finding some initial comfort from the beauty and meaningfulness of the service, the grief process was only beginning for the Treadaways. "I went very quickly from denial, to sorrow, to anger," Joel acknowledges. From there, unable to process his own feelings, let alone anyone else's, he withdrew from the family and began burying himself in his work. He accepted a number of out-of-town cases. One took him away from home for three weeks, another for 10 days.

"Suddenly I needed him, and he was never there," Lena says.

Joel says now, "It pains me to admit it, but I just quit nurturing my wife. I couldn't worry about her or my other children. It was selfishness on my part, but my number-one priority became me."

Joel was mad at God. Like the trial lawyer he was, Joel had a long list of cross-examination questions he wanted God to answer.

Through this time, Joel had a close Christian friend named Mike McIntyre who talked with him two or three times a week. They had been accountability partners for several years. One day Mike told Joel, "You know, what you're doing is running away. And as long as you're running, this problem is going to get bigger."

Joel's only outward reaction was to tell his friend, "That's interesting. I'll think about that." He didn't tell him until much later how mad Mike had made him by being so right.

But mostly, Joel was mad at God. Like the trial lawyer he was, Joel had a long list of cross-examination questions he wanted God to answer. *Why did*

You have to take Seth now? Were You just trifling with us by keeping him alive so long? Were we just too happy? Didn't You think we'd had enough pain? Didn't we do enough to justify having Seth? Did You expect us to pray harder or have more faith? Hearing no answers to any of those questions made Joel even angrier.

"I had all these feelings bottled up inside," he says, "like a Coke that is shaken and foaming and ready to explode. But my feelings had nowhere to go, because I'd closed myself off from God and my family."

Finally, one day in the spring of 1993, Joel found himself sitting in his friend Mike's car. The dark, stormy weather matched his mood as a driving rain tapped a staccato beat across the roof and windshield. After they talked for a time, Joel finally opened up his pain by praying, "God, we did the right thing when we took Seth in. We did what You asked us to do. And it's caused us so much pain. How could You do this? If You really love us, how can You ask us to go through this? How could You just take Seth like that?"

As the two men conversed, Mike reminded Joel of a number of truths he already knew: that God had created Seth and given him to Joel and Lena as a precious gift—the same way He had given them their other kids. That God was sovereign. That God knew exactly what it felt like to lose a son. That Joel still had another son and a daughter, while God had only one Son, and He'd been willing to give Him for us. "But even after I'd worked through all that," Joel says, "I was still thinking, *When I get to heaven, God had better be able to explain all this in a way I can understand!*"

Acknowledging he still wanted to believe God was ultimately in control didn't automatically make Joel *feel* it was true. But it was a first step that had to take place before there was any hope of restoring balance and peace in his life.

While Joel continued to pour his primary energies into his work, he knew he had to do something to help Lena and his children cope. So they scheduled a number of family trips in that first year after Seth's death. Being away from home meant they were away from some of the painful memories at Christmastime and spring break. For the same reason, Joel planned a family trip to the Grand Canyon to begin the summer of 1993.

The trouble was that Joel couldn't hide in his work on vacation, so his emotional withdrawal seemed even more painfully obvious. "On one level, the spectacular beauty of the Grand Canyon was a great distraction," he says. "We did a lot of hiking and other memorable activities with Danny and Sara.

But I don't know that I said 10 words to Lena the whole trip. That wasn't like me, at least not the old me. We all felt the tension. And it scared me. Somewhere I'd read that the great majority of couples who experience the loss of a child end up getting a divorce. I didn't want to be a part of those statistics.

"When we got home, Lena and I went out a few times to eat alone. But we still weren't connecting on an emotional level. I knew something needed to change. I knew *I* needed to change. I just couldn't figure out how. So I continued to throw myself into my work."

A friend invited Joel to Promise Keepers in Boulder. He declined, saying he had a trial starting that week. But when the case settled at the last minute, Joel called his friend back and said he'd go after all. He was desperate for answers; maybe he'd find some there.

When Joel got to Boulder and saw the program, he knew why it was that he had been meant to come. Dr. James Dobson, who had just published the book *When God Doesn't Make Sense*, was scheduled to speak on that subject the final night. *That's what I need to hear*, Joel thought, *because God hasn't been making a lot of sense to me lately*.

When the final session of the conference came and Dr. Dobson stepped to the microphone, however, he said, "I came prepared to talk to you about 'When God Doesn't Make Sense.' But I think there's something far more important than that. What I feel I need to talk to you about is 'What Your Wife Wants Me to Tell You.'"

Joel says, "It was as if he sat right down beside me and started pointing out what God, Mike, and Lena had been trying to tell me all along and I just hadn't been hearing. He talked about how a man who wants to be happy and healthy and everything God wants him to be needs to be making his wife and his wife's needs a priority. How God honors that. How we need to be careful to make sure our priorities reflect God's priorities for our lives."

The more Dobson talked, the bigger failure Joel realized he'd been. When his wife and family needed him most, he simply hadn't been there for them. They'd had to carry their own pain and grief without him. By the time Dobson finished, Joel was nearly overcome by guilt and remorse. He asked God to forgive him and help him get his life back in balance. And he vowed to do whatever it took to prove to his wife and children how important they were.

Joel flew home to Miami on Sunday morning. From the airport, he hurried right to church. "The moment I spotted Lena after the service, I grabbed hold of her and kissed her for what seemed like 15 minutes!" he says. "I just couldn't turn her loose. I guess she knew right then that something had happened!"

"Boy, did I!" Lena reports with a laugh. "Joel just wasn't a demonstrative person. He'd never think of kissing me in public. But whoa! This was a real kiss. We gathered quite a crowd of our friends—all watching and grinning.

"The look in Joel's eyes was so warm and loving. It was really something special. When he finally let go, I laughed and told him, 'You're going to Promise Keepers more often, Bud.' It clearly ranks as one of the most exciting moments of our lives, because Joel was declaring by his actions, 'Lena, I'm going to prove that I'm recommitting myself to you.'"

For nearly a year, Joel's withdrawal had kept Lena and their children from dealing with their own grief and questions regarding Seth's death. He now realized how much they all still had to work through. At Joel's suggestion, he and Lena read and discussed *When God Doesn't Make Sense*. He encouraged her to dump on him all the pain she'd bottled up for so long. He talked openly with Danny and Sara about their feelings and his. Together as a family, they would sometimes discuss some of their good memories of Seth.

As he reinvested himself in the everyday routine of his family and reestablished a healthy balance in his priorities, Joel began to get a perspective he hadn't had when everything got so out of whack. "As I focused on making my family a priority again," he says, "as I tried to fulfill Lena's and Danny's and Sara's needs, it began to dawn on me that Seth doesn't need me now, because he's in heaven. He's already enjoying what the rest of us will have to wait for. He's not sick anymore; he's just fine.

"It was Danny and Sara who needed me now. I was the only dad they had. They were entitled to my love, attention, and time. I was the only husband Lena had. She, too, needed to know she was a priority. And I'd have to work at making sure that happened."

Joel Treadaway continues to work as a trial lawyer, a career that routinely demands long, hard hours. But Lena says, "He's here for us now emotionally in ways he wasn't during those long months of withdrawal. When he's with us, he's really with us."

The Treadaways both acknowledge that keeping their priorities in healthy balance takes determination and planning. Every couple of weeks, Joel and Lena sit down with his work calendar and their family calendar to schedule upcoming events and responsibilities and resolve potential conflicts as far in advance as possible.

"There's some flexibility in everyone's job," Joel says. "So whenever possible, I work my schedule around the family things that can't be changed—like the kids' ball games and piano recitals. And once I get one of the kids' activities on my personal schedule, I treat it the same way I do a business meeting. It's no more acceptable for me to miss a family activity than it is to miss a business appointment."

Family trips and outings have become a regular highlight for the Treadaways again. They find there's nothing like concentrated blocks of time together—whether it's for a week or just a weekend—to help everyone feel the family is a priority.

Joel also recommends looking for ways to squeeze quality time out of ordinary family routines. He cites grocery shopping as an example. He does the family food purchasing every Saturday morning and says Danny and Sara always fight over whose turn it is to go with him. "It's amazing the kinds of things we've talked about while grocery shopping," Joel says.

Yet another way Joel proves to his family what a priority they are, Lena says, is by being the instigator, planner, and spark for family activities. Whether it's a ski trip to Colorado or just a kickball game with neighborhood kids in the backyard, he's usually the one who suggests the idea and then makes sure it happens.

Joel also puts a renewed emphasis on communication. "Some people may think it's strange," Lena says, "but we do a lot of our talking on the phone. Some days he's gone from home a lot of hours; so when he's home, we want him to spend as much time as he can with the kids. He's a morning person and I'm a night owl, so that adds to the challenge of finding time alone. That's why we end up talking on the phone once or twice every single day—whether he's in town or out."

Furthermore, Joel and Lena say they regularly pray as a family, as a couple, and as individuals. The result is a strong sense of feeling supported, of being important to each other.

Making family a priority sometimes requires compromises or sacrifices in other areas of life, as Joel has discovered. For example, he consistently turns down opportunities and responsibilities within his own law firm. He begs off internal committee assignments, explaining that with the demands of his practice and his family, his plate is more than full. "Our compensation is determined in part by the extent of our involvement in firm activities," he says. "So my not being so involved does cost me money." But evidently enough of Joel's colleagues respect his priorities that he continues to succeed professionally and as a partner in the firm.

For Joel, his reestablishment of priorities has certainly been worth it. After 20 years of marriage, he says, "Lena and I have a great relationship again. She's my best friend. If there's anyone in the world I wish I could spend more time with, it's her."

Lena adds, "For a time there, I thought our marriage was over. It may as well have been. But I have my husband back now. He's alive again. There's an intensity of love I haven't felt since our newlywed days. For a long time after Joel came home from Boulder, I kept waiting for his mountaintop glow to fade. But that glow has remained steady ever since. The balance we have yearned for is here. We can almost touch the peace."

Personal Evaluation

Review the following list of statements concerning you and your wife and marriage, and rate each one on a scale from 1 ("This is a serious problem") to 5 ("This is no problem at all"). If you're brave and you really want some helpful input, ask your wife to do the same exercise.

	Me	Wife
• We both work, and that's straining our relationship.	_____	_____
• I spend too many hours at work.	_____	_____
• We don't have enough money to pay all our bills each month.	_____	_____
• We've had a new child in the last 12 months.	_____	_____
• I travel a great deal for my work.	_____	_____
• My wife thinks I spend too much time at my hobby (golf, workshop, etc.).	_____	_____
• We've moved in the last 12 months.	_____	_____
• We disagree on where to worship.	_____	_____
• I have a lot of stress from my job.	_____	_____
• We disagree on how to discipline our children.	_____	_____
• We don't have enough quality time together.	_____	_____
• I spend too much time watching TV and/or reading the paper.	_____	_____
• The kids are grown and gone, and we seem to have drifted apart.	_____	_____
• The honeymoon is over, and marriage is more difficult than I expected.	_____	_____

Result interpretations:
1. If any number is a 1 or 2, that area needs attention.
2. If you and your wife differ by 2 or more points on any issue, you need to discuss it.

In the Group

1. What struggle with priorities did you identify in the "My Response" section of the preceding session? Have you seen any answer to your prayer yet? If so, what was it?

2. Think of the last major change you went through: new job, major move, loss of a loved one, and so on. How did it affect your ability to keep your priorities in order?

3. When Joel's son died, Joel cut himself off from God and his wife. His friend Mike helped him "wake up" and see the need to reconnect. When you're in a tough time, who can come alongside to help you? (If you can't identify someone, the time to start building such a friendship is *before* the crisis. Talk about how you can develop such relationships with each other in your group.)

4. What lessons can we learn from how and when Mike chose to confront his friend?

5. Read Psalm 40:1-3. How well do those verses capture Joel's feelings both before and after he started dealing with his son's death head-on?

6. What was the proof of Joel's new commitment to his family?

7. On a scale from 1 (not at all) to 10 (very closely), how emotionally connected are you to your wife? _____ How do you know that? What answer would she give? (If you're not married, answer these questions about your best friend.)

8. How does your wife (or the person closest to you if you're not married) tend to signal when all is not well in your relationship?

9. As Dr. James Dobson has observed, life boils down to whom you love and who loves you. What, if anything, is keeping your loved ones from having the place of priority they deserve in your life? What are you going to do about that?

My Response

Because of this session, one thing I need to do next week is _____

_____

Memory Verse

"Instead, speaking the truth in love, we will in all things grow up into him who is the Head, that is, Christ" (Eph. 4:15).

CHAPTER 5

Introduction

A Promise Keeper is committed to reaching beyond any denominational barriers to demonstrate the power of biblical unity. This aspect of living out our faith in everyday life is a giant promise!

There's an insecure and selfish core within each of us that screams, "I'm right, I'm better, and I'm afraid of what I don't understand." Only the power of the risen Christ can overcome this natural tendency.

One by one, Promise Keepers are winning the battle to defeat the enemy who sets up man against his brother. That sinister scheme to divide and conquer has left us fragmented, suspicious of one another, and isolated. But praise God, it's changing!

You'll be encouraged and inspired to read what God is doing in the lives of real men who have taken a risk to reach beyond formidable barriers.

A Promise Keeper Works for the Unity of All Christians

Although denominational loyalty isn't what it used to be in America, it's still common for people in one church to be at least a little suspicious of other kinds of Christians. Some denominations even continue to believe they alone are in the right with God. Ralph Heiss pastors a church in such a denomination, but God has made him a barrier breaker.

Ralph worked in retail sales until he was in his early thirties. He had a wife, Anna, two children, and a house in the suburbs. But he now admits, "Because I had a lot of exposure to the entertainment scene, I easily got into drugs. I got into an extramarital thing, too. My personal life was in shambles, and I knew it."

One day a woman acquaintance told Ralph about a Bible-preaching church her kids were attending only a couple of miles from his house. Ralph listened just to be polite, but afterward he couldn't get what she had said out of his mind. So on a Sunday morning a short time later, he got up and shocked his wife when he suggested, "Let's check this church out. I've heard some good things about it."

Ralph Heiss walked into a church that morning for the first time since he'd left his parents' home 15 years before. He had grown up in a church belonging to a large denomination, but he had never heard a clear gospel message. Although he felt there was something missing in his life, he didn't expect to find any answers in a church.

"But Anna and I walked into that church," he says, "and the sermon that day was one of the hottest messages on hell I've ever heard. I mean, this guy screamed and pointed his finger and spit. It was like some stereotype out of a movie. Yet God really broke my heart. And after that preacher got all done talking about hell, he said, 'Nobody has to go there. No matter how bad you've been, no matter what you've done, you can be forgiven.'

"He was really straight on that point, which was all new to me. I was raised with the philosophy that when you die, if the good you've done in life outweighs the bad, you'll go to heaven. The trouble was, over the years I'd come to the sobering conclusion that I would never be able to balance those scales. I'd made such a mess of my life that there wasn't anything I could do to break out of the downward spiral I was in. So I'd bought into the hedonistic attitude that I might as well have fun here on earth, because if there's a hell beyond, I'm gonna go there. There was just no way I could ever be the kind of person I wanted to be. No way I could even be the kind of good, moral man my father was. And I'd long since given up trying."

That's why the message about grace and forgiveness sounded good to Ralph—maybe too good. "My big problem was, it sounded so easy," he says. "How could anybody who had messed up as much as I had pray a simple prayer and have it all taken care of? So I hedged for a while, wrestling with my doubts, thinking, *It sounds good, but it can't be this simple!*"

About three weeks later, at the close of another service, Ralph and Anna walked together down the aisle of that church. And that same evening, they went home, got down on their knees beside the bed, and prayed and wept. The joy of salvation overwhelmed them.

"Without anyone telling us we should do it, we prayed a prayer of dedication together," Ralph says. "That prayer changed our lives forever, because we gave the Lord everything we had. We gave Him our home, our jobs, our kids. We just gave Him our lives and said, 'Lord, we don't know the magnitude of this, but whatever You want of our lives, they are Yours.' "

The very next week, God called Ralph to preach. "I was in a service," he says, "we were singing, and I was overwhelmed with the love of God. I couldn't stop crying. I just sat there, and it was like something kept saying, 'Life's not over. Make the rest of it count. Do something. Tell other people.' And I had this overwhelming desire to preach the gospel."

Some people tried to talk Ralph out of it. His pastor said, "You ought to wait a while and see how it goes as a Christian."

"I don't want to wait," Ralph told him. "I've wasted more than 30 years of my life already."

Ralph gave his notice at work. He stayed through the busy Christmas season, but in January, he moved his family to another state and began classes at a small Bible college affiliated with his new denomination. He remembers, "Our house hadn't sold, and I had no income. But I was a veteran, so I had the GI Bill coming, and God was faithful. I worked, my wife worked, the GI Bill money finally came, and we got by."

During his last year of school, Ralph was invited to pastor a little country church. He had been saved just two years earlier, and now he was pastoring. He didn't know why the church even wanted him but figured they couldn't get anybody else to take the job.

Ralph Heiss was an enthusiastic new preacher who believed everybody needed to hear the gospel. His little church saw 75 accept Jesus as Lord the first year he was there. The church's baptistery hadn't had water in it for three years, but Ralph baptized 50 people that first year, and the congregation tripled in size.

As a natural outgrowth of this revival, many newcomers of various backgrounds began attending the church. One young woman from a different denominational and theological persuasion wanted to join. Ralph expressed some concern about their disparities in belief. She acknowledged those differences but reassured him by saying, "I'd never hurt you, pastor. You're a man of God, and I've seen the hand of God on your ministry here."

The woman was such a zealous leader, however, that when she joined the church, many people were drawn to her. Without Ralph's knowledge, she began a Bible study in her home where a dozen or so new converts met each week to be taught by a woman she invited from another city. Before long, some of the members of that group were chastising Ralph for not teaching the same ideas they were learning in their Bible study.

Eventually that entire group and a number of others left the church, hurting and angering Ralph, who says, "I was young in the ministry, and this controversy nearly destroyed me, my ministry, and my family."

Some church members who stayed second-guessed their pastor's stand. They thought he should have been more accommodating to those who left. Others, long-time members for whom this was the first serious conflict in their congregation's memory, wanted to turn back the clock: "It was better here when it was just us, before all these new people started coming. This is our church, after all."

Months passed, and Ralph grew discouraged and began thinking the Lord must have some other place for him to serve. So without any other prospects, he turned in his resignation. As Ralph recalls, "The night I resigned, I went home and thought about what I had done. I was lying in bed beside my wife when I started to cry. Anna asked, 'What's the matter?' I said, 'Honey, we've got 30 days and then we don't have a roof over our heads.' I felt so defeated."

That experience reinforced everything others in Ralph's denomination believed about associating with other churches or people with different spiritual backgrounds. It seemed to validate all the warnings he had heard in Bible school. He had tried to be tolerant, only to feel as if he'd been burned for his openness and accommodation.

> ### Ralph routinely turned down all such invitations because, he says, "they weren't believers of my stripe."

In the wake of that experience, Ralph and Anna decided to move back to his home state of Ohio and begin an inner-city church. It proved to be demanding work. He took a job to help support his family, garnered some initial funding from other congregations in his denomination, rented a back room of another church, printed fliers, and began knocking on doors throughout his new neighborhood.

The church grew slowly but steadily. A couple of years passed, and the little congregation bought a big neighborhood house to meet in. A few years later, the church put up a new building in a racially mixed neighborhood. Ralph now pastors an integrated church with attendance running around 150.

Soon after Ralph began this church, a number of area pastors from various denominations reached out to invite him to join a fellowship of the city's evangelical clergy. They met every month to encourage one another and occasionally worked together in cooperative efforts like a local crusade. But Ralph routinely turned down all such invitations because, he says, "they weren't believers of my stripe. I'd make excuses, but what I really wanted to say to them was 'Just leave me alone.' "

According to Ralph, this was part of what he calls a hard-core exclusivist mind-set among the pastors in his denomination. That mind-set includes, among other things, "absolute pastoral authority, very strict standards on hair length and dress, and a very narrow range of acceptable music. It's a whole package."

When the subject of this evangelical pastors' group came up, one of Ralph's denominational colleagues said, "I don't even want to meet them, because I might like them. Then I might have to make some decisions I don't want to have to make."

The truth was, while Ralph went along with what he called "this isolationist attitude that we're right and everyone else in the world is wrong," he didn't personally buy into or preach the "whole package." Because of his background and the inner-city nature of his ministry, he was more tolerant regarding appearance and dress than most of his colleagues. He'd witnessed some abuses of pastoral authority that troubled him, too. And he was a lot more open-minded about music; some of his fellow clergy banned all accompaniment tapes for their church musicians because they deemed any music with a back-beat inappropriate in church. And in what was perhaps the most radical departure from his denomination's teaching, Ralph's didn't require everyone transferring membership from another denomination to resubmit to baptism in his church.

Ralph didn't do anything to broadcast his departure from the denominational standards, however. "In fact," Ralph says, "it sometimes felt like I was leading two lives. I followed my own convictions with my own congregation, but when I got together with fellow pastors for denominational gatherings, I was careful never to say or do anything to tip my hand. I went along because this was the only group I knew, the people who accepted me. And I depended on that acceptance.

"My denominational colleagues were like my family. In a human analogy, by going against accepted standards, I felt like a family member going out, falling in love, getting married to someone from the wrong side of the tracks, and then being afraid to let that love be known for fear of what my family would do to me. While I didn't agree with them on everything, I loved them and wanted them to love me. So even though there were sometimes things I felt I ought to do or say, I didn't, because it would have exposed me."

It was indirectly because of his denomination's attitude toward other

Christian groups that Ralph first heard about Promise Keepers. Bernie, an active member of a nearby congregation of Ralph's denomination, learned about the Boulder conference and decided he wanted to recruit other members of his church to go with him. But Bernie's pastor told him, "It's not our denomination. We're not interested."

Bernie went anyway. And when he returned, he couldn't say enough about the experience. His pastor told him he didn't want to hear anything about it, and because of Bernie's "disobedience" in going, he actually stripped him of his leadership roles in the church and suggested he move his membership to another congregation. The pastor recommended Ralph's church but then called to warn Ralph against giving Bernie any leadership responsibilities.

Ralph was so impressed with Bernie's spiritual commitment, however, that he soon disregarded his fellow pastor's advice. And when Bernie wanted to go hear a singer/evangelist he'd heard about through Promise Keepers, Ralph went with him.

As Ralph tells it, "This musician had played in the NFL, and he was a really dynamic preacher and singer, an awesome black brother. I was so impressed that I helped get him into the public schools to give drug talks to students. We talked quite a bit, and he challenged me. He said, 'Pastor Heiss, I believe if you'll take 10 men from your congregation to Promise Keepers, your church will never be the same.'"

With that encouragement, Ralph made a conscious decision to learn what Promise Keepers was all about. He sent away for a videotape of the message E.V. Hill preached at the Boulder conference.

His reaction? "It was hot! It was an inspired message. I showed it to our church to get them psyched about Promise Keepers, and 12 men signed up to go to the Indianapolis conference in June 1994."

Bernie had told him what to expect. So Ralph went to the conference anticipating a terrific lineup of speakers who would have a powerful impact on the dozen men of his church. What he never expected was the impact the experience would have on *him*.

It started during a song. Sixty thousand men in the Hoosier Dome stood and sang "Holy, Holy, Holy." "There were all kinds of guys," Ralph says, "from so many different church backgrounds, with all sorts of expressions—some with their hands raised and looking toward heaven, others with their eyes closed and their heads bowed. And it hit me, *Each one of us in his own way is lifting his heart to God. We're not doing anything sinful here. We're doing some-thing wonderful and beautiful."*

Later, at mealtime, those 60,000 men emptied out of the Hoosier Dome onto the streets of downtown Indianapolis. The massive lunch line packed the tunnel where the street passes under the train tracks running into Union Station next door. Somewhere in that huge, surging sea of humanity, some-body started to sing. Within moments, there was a spontaneous song service, with thousands of male voices echoing through the tunnel.

Ralph went to Promise Keepers anticipating a powerful impact on the men of his church. What he never expected was the impact the experience would have on him.

"It was truly one of the most beautiful things I have ever seen or heard," recalls Ralph. "And I couldn't help thinking, *This is just what heaven's going to be like. There's going to be a whole bunch of people who never knew each other, who have different doctrines and different skin colors and different preferences—all just focused on Jesus."*

Ralph was also impressed by the fact that in that huge, hungry crowd of strangers, he saw no pushing, no shoving, nobody getting impatient, every-body excited, but everyone being gracious.

"Then there was a handful of protesters outside with signs saying 'Jesus is not God' and all sorts of anti-Christian slogans," he says. "I particularly remember one guy wearing a pin that said 'Ex-fundamentalist inside.' I suspect if the tables had been turned, if 60,000 atheists had come out of the Hoosier Dome to find eight or 10 protesters, some people would have died that day. Instead, the Promise Keepers crowd handed these protesters tracts, told them they loved them, invited them inside, and sang to them. And I think that just blew the protesters away. They evidently couldn't deal with it, because the next thing I knew, they had just sort of melted away and were gone."

When the conference started again, Ralph suddenly realized he had been wrong in the way he was treating other Christians. "And I knew without a doubt," he says, "that the first thing I needed to do when I got home was to go to that group of evangelical pastors I'd snubbed for 15 years and apologize for my intolerant attitude."

When he returned home, Ralph discovered that the next meeting of the pastors' group would be held in less than a week. So after 15 years of spurned invitations, Ralph showed up for his first luncheon. There were only a couple of men he even recognized. But before the meeting began, he searched out the group's presiding officer, introduced himself, and said, "This may sound like a strange request. I'm not a member of this organization, and I really have no right to be heard, but I believe God told me to come and apologize to this group. If you'll give me a minute, I'd like to do that. I won't say anything harmful or embarrassing to anybody; I just feel impressed by God to come and make this right."

So after the meal, the man gave Ralph the floor. He stepped to the podium, told the group who he was, what church he pastored, and simply said, "A lot of you don't even know who I am. But I just got back from Promise Keepers over in Indianapolis, and the Lord has dealt with me about my attitude toward all of you. I've been wrong. I just wanted to ask if you would please forgive me. I want to do better."

According to Ralph, "When I walked back to my seat, it seemed as if the group was in a state of shock. I guess what I said made an impact, because in the months since, several pastors have come up to me and said, 'Wow! I was at that meeting when you apologized to the group. That was something!' But I didn't do it to make any kind of impact. I did it because when you tell God you're going to do something, you've got to do it. I was just grateful for the opportunity."

Some months later, the pastors' group met to discuss the possibility of having a Promise Keepers conference in their area. Instead of the usual 25 or 30 attendees, 150 showed up. Ralph was introduced to give a brief testimony about Promise Keepers. When he told the group what denomination he belonged to, he said, "Most of you know what that means. It means I'm right and you're all wrong. But I went to Promise Keepers this past summer and realized that the attitude I've had my entire ministry toward other Christians has been wrong. Promise Keepers has taught me that you are all my brothers. I can finally say I love you. I want to work with you, and we need to bring Promise Keepers to our city because other people need to experience what's happening through this movement of God."

That was all Ralph said. But the ramifications of that little testimony are still spreading. A few weeks later, Ralph accepted an invitation to an organizational luncheon to discuss plans for an area-wide evangelistic outreach that would distribute video copies of the "Jesus" film to every home in the county.

"Ours is a big county, so it's going to take a lot of cooperation," Ralph says. "But it's so exciting. And to think that before, I'd never have dreamed of being involved because this was too inclusive! I would have been so afraid to be seen with those people. But now I'm committed to crossing lines with other believers. I firmly believe we can find a basis for true fellowship in our salvation through the Lord Jesus Christ."

However, Ralph is beginning to realize what his change in attitude may cost him. Some of the pastors within his denomination have taken note of his activities. "I recently talked to one of my long-time colleagues about riding with him to a denominational meeting," Ralph says. "He told me he'd get back to me to work out our plans, but he never did. And I just learned that another colleague's church is planning a big celebration for the twenty-fifth anniversary of the congregation's founding, and I'm the only local pastor from our denomination who hasn't been invited to participate.

"I have to admit that hurts. There's so much potential in our denomination, so many good things God has already done through it. I have to come back to the family analogy and confess that I desperately long for the love and approval of my denominational family."

Nonetheless, Ralph is at peace with who he is and where he now stands. "To do anything less or different would be unfaithful to God," he asserts. "Yet I don't want to portray myself as some kind of martyr. And I'm certainly no saint. I make plenty of mistakes, and I do lots of stupid things. But this is one area of my ministry where I know God has told me what He wants me to do.

"I haven't changed my own basic beliefs," he continues. "So I don't agree with everything my new evangelical brothers believe. But we can agree on the core issues and accept each other's differences on the nonessentials. I don't believe any of us is ever going to understand it all till we get to heaven anyway. And at that point, we're not going to care. It'll all be straightened out. There'll be one Lord, one doctrine, no denominations, no names, and that'll be good. In the meantime, I see Promise Keepers as heaven rehearsal— getting us ready to get along for all eternity. There's just so little that separates us, so much that should unite us, and so much work to be done."

Personal Evaluation

What denominations or types of Christians have you tended to look down on in the past? Why?

In the Group

1. Based on the discussion in the previous two sessions, what changes have you made regarding your priorities? What changes do you still need to make?
2. When thousands of men go to a Promise Keepers conference, they seem to worship and learn together without worrying about denominational labels. Why is that? How can that dynamic be transferred to the local community?
3. Is it possible for Christians to have different views on issues like spiritual gifts or acceptable musical styles and still get along together in the same church? Why or why not?
4. What do you think Jesus meant in John 17 when He prayed for unity among His followers? What's the difference between biblical unity and uniformity?
5. How can we make practical application of John 13:34-35 to this issue of getting along as Christian brothers?
6. Generally speaking, are the issues that divide Christians man-made or God-directed? Explain your reasoning. Upon what core beliefs should we come together?
7. What biblical and practical steps might you as individuals take to start breaking down some denominational barriers? as a small group? as a church?

My Response

One individual or group that I believe God might want me to approach across a denominational barrier is _____

A first step I can take in the near future is_____

Memory Verse

"I in them and you in me. May they be brought to complete unity to let the world know that you sent me and have loved them even as you have loved me" (John 17:23).

CHAPTER 6

Introduction

Just as Promise Keepers is committed to breaking down denominational barriers between Christian men while still celebrating our rich denominational heritage, it's also dedicated to promoting reconciliation among Christian men of all ethnic and cultural backgrounds. But how does that come about? How do we move from good intentions to God-honoring action?

David, Fred, and Jim are three men in their thirties. One is black; two are white. All are committed Christians. And the way their lives have come together gives us one example of how reconciliation can move from rhetoric to reality.

A Promise Keeper Pursues
Racial Reconciliation

Born in 1956, David Tibbet grew up in the inner city of Detroit. "My father taught me about character and how to get along in the world," he says. "My mom taught me how to love and care for people."

David doesn't remember the first time he consciously considered the color of his own brown skin. He does remember watching TV as a child and wondering, *Why are all the black people so dark?* At the age of six, he got into a fight for calling one of his best buddies *black* because the boy's skin was a darker shade than his own.

"I didn't have much personal contact with anyone from other racial or ethnic backgrounds," David recalls. "My father was into boxing. So he and his friends used to compare fighters like Sugar Ray Robinson and Rocky Marciano. They'd talk about Irish boxers being slow and Hispanic fighters having jaws of concrete so you had to pummel them, and still you couldn't knock them out. I knew without anyone telling me that people like that were different from me."

David's father drove a truck for the city of Detroit. All the men on his crew were black. White truck drivers worked with all-white crews. And most of them would be gone by the time David's dad got back to the garage in the evenings. "Even at the age of six or seven, I noticed and thought that kind of odd," David says.

Experiencing the riots of 1967 and seeing National Guard tanks rolling down the street past his home underlined racial distinctions in a new way for 11-year-old David. So did his selection the following year for a special, six-week-long, summer academic program called Horizons Upward Bound, which was held on the campus of a private boarding school in the ritzy suburb of Bloomfield Hills. David and the other kids in that program quickly learned the boundaries beyond which they couldn't comfortably go. If they wandered off campus, some white person would invariably ask, "What are you guys doing here?" Store owners clearly noticed and watched when they walked in.

"No one called me ugly names," David says. "It was more subtle than that. But I got the clear message I didn't belong."

Not that all his exposure to whites was negative. He was selected as a student representative of Upward Bound to attend a special dinner in the Bloomfield Hills home of one of the program's patrons. "The people were very nice, and the dinner was elegant," David remembers. "That was the first and only time I ever ate venison." And then there was the suburban white couple who somehow got matched up with the Tibbets when David's family was going through financial struggles in his early teen years. "They sent money every month for a couple of years to help purchase my school supplies and clothes," he says. "I also visited their home one time during the second year."

> *Even his positive interactions seemed to underscore the differences between David's black experience and the broader white world.*

But even those positive interactions seemed to underscore the differences between David's black experience and the broader white world. "The biggest difference by far seemed to be economic," he says.

To help support his family, David worked a full-time evening job the last couple years of high school. Through those difficult days, he never gave up his long-time dream of becoming an architect. But after his grades slipped the first semester before he learned to juggle his work and school schedules, the white guidance counselor at his college-prep high school discouraged his application to the University of Michigan's architecture school. Instead, she directed him toward a less-demanding local college. "From talking to friends later, I learned she'd encouraged a lot of other African-American students to lower their academic goals, too," David says. Whether that was conscious racism or simply poor counseling, she didn't seem to have the same approach with the white students. Her advice ultimately cost David two years in the pursuit of his dream.

In the course of college and architecture school, David remembers interacting and even developing friendships with students of various ethnic backgrounds. But for the most part, he did what everyone else did—gravitated toward fellow students of his own race. And the prejudice he encountered was usually subtle and unspoken.

One memorable exception came during his time in architecture school, where David first earned a teaching fellowship and then landed another job doing architectural drawing in the design office of one of his professors. "He was a kindly older gentleman I really enjoyed working for," David says. "One of the projects I helped him with was the expansion and remodeling of a popular restaurant. One day, after the job was completed, he asked if I'd like to drive with him to see the finished product. We had a nice conversation during the ride, but when we arrived at the restaurant and climbed out of the car, he told me the owner was very prejudiced. He asked if I'd be willing to wait outside and just look through the window at the interior. I was so surprised that I simply said, 'Sure.' He went in, talked to the owner for a few minutes, came back out, and we drove home."

> **Personal evaluation:** How would you have felt if you had been left outside the restaurant you had helped design? What might have happened if the professor had taken David in and introduced him with honor as a colleague in the project?

"At the time," David continues, "I angrily resented that owner's attitude. But as the years passed and I'd look back on that experience, I became more and more disappointed in my professor. I'd thought he respected and liked me. But either he wasn't sensitive enough to foresee how offensive the experience would be, or he didn't care enough to stand up with me against his client's bigotry. Either way, it made me wonder where else I could expect to encounter prejudice when I left school and ventured out into corporate America."

If that kind of experience, added to a lifetime of witnessing the economic differences between the majority of blacks and the majority of whites, didn't make David bitter, it at least made him cynical. It also made him question what he heard people say about God's love.

He began dating a girl named Connie during college. After they graduated, he asked her to marry him. But she told him no because he wasn't a Christian at the time, and she didn't think she should be "unequally yoked."

"Wait a minute, sweetheart," he told her. "We're not oxen, you know."

David had heard the gospel all his life, but believing it enough to base his life on it wasn't easy. He kept asking, "If God is such a loving God, why does He have black people as disenfranchised as we are in the United States? Why are we having it so tough?"

Then one day, when David and Connie's brother-in-law were jogging together, David says, "He helped me understand that the Christian life is a one-on-one relationship, not a group exercise. I can remember the exact spot on the road where we stopped, he quoted John 3:16, and I finally understood and accepted Christ."

But as David began to grow in the faith, he still wrestled with the existence of racism and the economic disparity between blacks and whites—even between black and white churches. It took time to come to the point of truly believing God is in ultimate control. "It particularly bothered me to realize that in our American culture, Sunday morning from 11:00 to 12:00 remains one of the most, if not *the* most, segregated hours of the week."

In recent years, however, David has begun to find hope for Christian unity between brothers of different races. This, too, has occurred on a personal level.

When he took a job with his current company in Dallas, Texas, six years ago, David was assigned office space kitty-corner to that of an architect named Mark Turkington. By the second or third day, the two men realized they were both Christians and gradually began sharing details about their families and backgrounds. One grew up in inner-city Detroit. The other was reared on a Nebraska farm. Yet these two Christian brothers soon became friends—and more. "Right now, Mark and I are accountability partners," David says. "We take one lunch a week together to go through some formal accountability questions. *What's happening in your relationship with God? What has He taught you this past week? How are you doing in terms of loving your wife? How are you doing as a father? Are you maintaining a pure heart?* And the last question we ask one another, *Have you been completely honest in answering my questions?*

"We've learned to love and trust one another enough to be totally vulnerable. We pray together and for each other. We share our deepest secrets and feelings. Mark's one of my two best friends. We've had some differences we've had to work through—as you do in any relationship. But our racial differences are merely a fact of our lives, not a hindrance to our friendship. I've come a long way since the time I almost rejected Christianity because of the racial differences I saw in the world."

> ## *"Our racial differences are merely a fact of our lives, not a hindrance to our friendship."*

David also sees how his experience as an African American has prepared him to be a father for his three children, especially his youngest son, who has Down's syndrome. "I believe that by letting me see and experience injustice firsthand, God has made me uniquely qualified to be the father of a child the world will always see and treat as different."

Fred VanderMay grew up on a west Texas farm with what he calls "a heritage of prejudice that goes back for generations in my family—prejudice against Hispanics and blacks."

He remembers his mother and grandmothers often hiring Mexican-American women to help do household work because "you can always get a Mexican to do it cheaper."

The first time he consciously recognized racial differences came in second grade, when he made friends at school with a black boy named Sam. They became inseparable, always playing together at recess and sitting next to each other in class. One evening around the VanderMay family dinner table, the subject of friends came up, and Fred announced, "Sammy is my very best friend."

He remembers his parents' response: "They didn't say anything, but I noticed the way they looked at each other—a little alarmed and embarrassed."

Later that same evening, as Fred was going to bed, his mother drew him aside from his brothers to say, "I'm sure Sammy has been a good friend to you. But you need to find other friends. He should probably be someone else's friend in the future."

Fred says, "It wasn't so much her words as the attitude that said, *He's not good enough for you; he's different.* I knew exactly what she meant."

Starting the next day, Fred began making new friends and simply snubbed Sammy. He couldn't help noticing the look of confusion and hurt on

Sammy's face. "I felt torn inside," he says. "But I told myself, *I'm not supposed to be his friend. He isn't good enough for me.*" From then on, the two boys went their separate ways.

> **Personal evaluation:** On a scale from 1 (virtually none) to 10 (a great deal), how much racism do you think you harbor in your heart? On what do you base that conclusion? What can you do to push your score closer to a 1?

There weren't a lot of blacks where Fred grew up. The most frequent targets of racism were Hispanics. "The term 'dirty Mexcan' was a frequent part of west Texas vocabulary," Fred admits. "And it was always 'Mex-can' rather than 'Mex-i-can.'"

The majority of students at Fred's high school had Hispanic heritage. Yet he says he never considered himself in the minority: "I was white, after all." He knew and got along well with many Hispanic kids at school—competing with them in sports, playing in the band with them, belonging to the same honor society, and serving together on the student council. But those relationships always seemed to begin and end at school.

An exception took place one day when a group of guys Fred hung out with walked to his house for lunch. He'd offered the spur-of-the-moment invitation without stopping to realize one of the guys was Hispanic. "I remember feeling uncomfortable the whole time he was at my house," Fred says. He continued to be friends with that boy and other Hispanics at school. But the experience reinforced the lesson in his mind: "It was clearly more comfortable for all concerned to stick with people of their own race. I never thought that was a matter of prejudice so much as it seemed simple common sense. It was just the way things were."

Fred certainly didn't consider himself bigoted. He even dated a Hispanic girl during college, though he never could forget their ethnic differences—at least for long. First it was his parents' disapproval: "We trust you aren't going to get serious with her. Surely you'll find another girlfriend soon."

The girl, too, kept reminding him of their differences. When they argued or she got upset about something, she'd say things like "You're too good for that—you're a white boy" or "You wouldn't understand because you live on the other side of town."

"I saw in her bitterness, for the first time, the deep pain caused by racial and ethnic divisions," Fred says.

In many ways, Fred left his roots and broadened his perspective during his college years. He told himself his education and exposure to fellow students of many races during his medical-school days gave him a more enlightened viewpoint. As a committed Christian, he recognized as sin the kind of overt bigotry he'd seen in his family. But he didn't consider himself prejudiced anymore—if he ever was.

When he went to the Promise Keepers 1993 conference in Boulder, however, Fred became convicted by the speakers who talked about the need for Christian men to knock down the racial barriers that divide America. He realized that even though he thought he was free of the blatant intolerance that had been part of his cultural background, many barriers remained. At least in part, that was because he didn't really know or interact on a meaningful level with anyone of another race.

In response to the challenge, when Fred returned home to Dallas, he organized a Promise Keepers group of five men that included two blacks. "If I was going to knock down the racial barriers in my life," he says, "I knew I would need to understand from these two men their culture, their pain, and their love for Christ."

One of the men made an immediate impact on Fred. "I remember the first time we got together and I listened to Ernest talk," Fred says. "He began by shaking his head and saying, 'Oh, if my father could only see me now. This is something I have only dreamed of—to be able to share and pray with a white man.'

"And as Ernest began to reveal his heart, he started to cry. He told about the tough home life he had as a kid and how the military provided him an escape. He'd had a substance-abuse problem for years before he found Christ. Now in his forties, he's a full-time counselor in a state hospital drug-rehab program. But he admitted he continues to struggle with the painful consequences of his past sins. His wife had divorced him when he was doing drugs and alcohol. So for years now, he's been working for reconciliation with the children he feels he failed as a father.

"The entire time Ernest talked, I felt like a little boy being led by the hand as this strong man of God opened up and showed me the power of Christ's love in his life. It created a longing in me to understand and spend more time with other minority men."

But it soon became evident that not everyone in Fred's small group felt the same. The other two white men dropped out. One of them as much as admitted he just didn't feel ready to share his heart with men of another race. But even after the little group disbanded, Fred continued to meet one on one with Ernest and the second black man, Charles, who was the pastor of a local church.

According to Fred, it was an enriching as well as an enlightening exposure to the culture of these two new friends: "To hear their stories; to see how God was working in their lives; to learn how they struggled with so many of the things I did; to understand their need to feel accepted and loved; to see how much we had in common. The experience worked on my heart for the entire year. Then I invited Ernest to go with me and my brother-in-law Carl to the 1994 Promise Keepers conference in Denton, Texas."

Jim O'Toole's Irish Catholic family lived in Dallas when he was growing up in the sixties and seventies. His parents had grown up in northern Mississippi. Jim remembers that his first and clearest exposure to racism came on his annual trips to visit grandparents and other extended family there. "The men would make crude, racist jokes about black athletes as we watched sports on television," Jim says. "And I vividly recall some of the really ugly comments made after Martin Luther King, Jr., was killed. There always seemed to be an undertone of racial hatred."

Jim doesn't remember his parents ever directly contradicting or even discussing the bigotry he heard from other relatives. But they certainly never espoused such bigotry themselves. In fact, when the Dallas public school system began a pilot busing program, a first step toward true integration, the O'Tooles chose to participate. Jim's parents took all three of their kids out of parochial grade school to be among 30 North Dallas students bused into the inner city to attend a formerly all-black school.

They didn't ever talk directly about the reasons for their decision, but they obviously felt it was the right thing to do. "As far as I remember," Jim says, "that was my first real exposure to people of a different race. I remember thinking that year was an exciting and fun experience. I never thought twice about being a white student in a mostly black environment. I was just going to a new school."

Jim continued in public school all the way through the twelfth grade. And since his high school was about 40 percent white, 40 percent black, and 20 percent Hispanic, he regularly interacted with students of varying backgrounds. But none of them became close friends.

There was a black friend in junior high, however, who invited Jim to an evangelistic service where he first heard the gospel presented in a way that made sense. He responded to that message and was baptized a short while later.

But Jim's faith didn't really grow until he got involved in a singles ministry after college and began attending a Sunday school class that consistently studied the Bible. It was at that point that Jim met and married his wife, Alice, who'd recently become a Christian through the influence of a college friend who, in turn, met and married Fred VanderMay. The two couples maintained a friendship over the years.

Jim and Alice eventually had a baby daughter. Three years later, Alice got pregnant again and had a son, Andrew, who was born with multiple birth defects. Among the people they contacted to pray for their son were the VanderMays and a friend Jim knew from a Bible study group he attended—Mark Turkington.

Mark made plans during his lunch hour the next day to visit Jim at the hospital where Andrew remained in serious condition. As Mark was leaving the office, his friend David Tibbet caught him in the hall. "Want to grab lunch somewhere together?" David asked. When Mark explained where he was going, David said, "I've got no plans. Mind if I tag along?"

Jim takes up the story. "I'd never met David before," he says. "But when he walked into that hospital waiting room and Mark introduced us, I felt like I'd known him all my life. He shook my hand and warmly congratulated me for having a son. In the two days since Andrew's birth, there had been so much concern about his medical problems that no one had ever really congratulated me. David was the first."

As the three men walked from the waiting room to the intensive-care unit (ICU) to see Andrew, David said, "Sons are truly wonderful gifts from the Lord."

Jim thought, *Finally someone who understands!* And he responded, "You're exactly right. My son *is* a gift."

The men prayed for Andrew and then talked for a while. When David mentioned his son with Down's syndrome, Jim understood the reason for the special connection he felt with his new acquaintance. "Because he, too, had a son the world sees as different," Jim says, "he could look at my son with understanding eyes.

"Andrew's legs were twisted, and his spine had a severe curvature. The doctors weren't sure he'd ever walk—if he even continued to live. He had serious heart problems as well. From the outside looking in, most people saw only a deformed child. David was able to see a special gift, a child made in God's image. He was able to do that, and help give me that same view, because he sees his own son the same way."

But the O'Tooles' ordeal had only begun. To date, their son has gone through seven surgeries (two on his legs, three on his abdomen, and two on his heart) plus another handful of serious procedures (including four heart catheterizations). At several points, Andrew slipped to the verge of death.

Whenever his son needed special prayer, Jim would call Mark, who would then call the other men in their Bible study. If Mark wasn't at his desk, Jim would allow the phone to bounce back to the switchboard and ask to speak to David. "All three of us got together a couple times for lunch," Jim says. "But over those next few months, my only regular contact with David was limited to those phone calls. Even so, our friendship began to deepen and grow."

A year or so after Andrew was born, David joined the same Bible study group Mark and Jim belonged to. And they've been getting together a couple of times every week since. "More than three years have passed since Andrew was born," Jim says. "He's able to get around on a walker now, continuing to amaze the doctors with his progress. And over this long, difficult time, David and I have become special friends by encouraging each other as fathers and praying for each other's son. There's nothing I wouldn't do for him."

> ### On the day after Andrew was born, Dr. Takenaka went through the treatment options with Jim and his wife. The chances were not good no matter what course they chose.

But David Tibbet hasn't been the only person of color important in the O'Tooles' life these past few years. The pediatric heart specialist who cared for Andrew grew up in Japan. On the day after Andrew was born, Dr. Takenaka went through the treatment options with Jim and his wife, explaining the various procedures and the success rate for each. The chances were not good no matter what course they chose, so the doctor honestly told them the time might soon come when they would have to decide what was best *for* Andrew and not what was best to do *to* him.

Jim looked at Dr. Takenaka and said, "Doctor, we're Christians, and we believe God has a plan for Andrew's life. We don't know if he's going to live seven days, seven weeks, or seventy years. That's not in our hands. We understand there may come a time when we have to let him go."

They talked a little longer, and then Dr. Takenaka got up to leave. But before he reached the door, he turned and said in his halting English, "I Christian, too." Then he bowed, turned again, and walked from the room.

Jim was heartened to know Andrew's doctor looked to God. The doctor's words before each surgery, when he'd come to take Andrew to the operating room, also reassured Jim. "I go do best job," he'd say. "You go pray." And whenever anyone tried to thank him or praise his special gifts, the doctor's humble response would always be the same: "These just human hands. Takes God to use these hands to heal."

For the six weeks Andrew remained on a respirator, his (and his parents') favorite nurse was a Hispanic woman named Lita. One of the respiratory therapists who always took special care with Andrew was a Hispanic man named Angel.

The day after his first open-heart surgery, Andrew stopped breathing three different times. The third time sounded a code blue alarm, and medical staff came running from all over the hospital. The doctor who helped revive Andrew that time was from India.

In that same day, one of the medical technicians in the ICU, a black woman named Vanessa, pulled a chair into a corner of the room away from all the commotion surrounding the baby. There she sat down and prayed until he was out of danger. "She wouldn't leave until she knew Andrew was okay," says Jim.

And then there was a Hispanic friend of a friend who showed up unannounced before one of Andrew's surgeries to volunteer as a blood donor. They already had nine units of blood on hand, and Raphael's made 10. During and after the surgery, Andrew required all 10. "If Raphael hadn't donated, Andrew might have died," says Jim.

In June 1994, Jim O'Toole made last-minute plans to attend the Promise Keepers conference in Denton. He went by himself because he hadn't been able to connect with anyone else he knew was going.

During one of the breaks in the program, however, Jim literally bumped into his friend Fred VanderMay walking around the stadium track. Fred was there with his twin brother, Frank, his friend Ernest, and Fred's brother-in-law Carl, who had just committed his life to Christ in one of the morning sessions.

Jim decided to sit in the stands with Fred's group for the next session. They listened carefully as Tony Evans preached about how God wants to change one man at a time. A changed man can change his family, Evans said. Changed families can change a neighborhood. Changed neighborhoods can change a community. Changed communities can change cities, which can change states, which can change the nation, which can change the world. What God wants, Evans declared, is one man at a time who is willing to start making a difference. And he asked for men to come forward who were willing to step out and make a difference—particularly men who wanted to knock down the racial walls in their lives, to reach out to men of all colors. He asked anyone who felt he needed to confess racism or ill will toward any brother to come forward and do that.

As Jim listened to that invitation, his friend Fred bolted out of the stands. Fred's brother Frank was only a step behind. Their brother-in-law Carl seemed to hesitate a moment or two, taking a step and stopping, then taking another step and stopping again. Finally, he, too, hurried to the front of the platform at the end of the stadium.

As Fred tells it, "When Tony Evans spoke about the need for racial reconciliation, I began to cry. I thought of all I'd learned from and about the pain my black friends Ernest and Charles had experienced. I felt a weight of guilt for all that I'd done and not done over the years to ostracize minorities and not let them even be a part of my life—starting with my friend Sammy and continuing all my life. For all those years there had been no sharing, no fellowship with brothers of different races.

"When Tony asked for men who were ready to change that, I rushed forward for a time of confession and commitment. There were two black men in the crowd around the platform who prayed with me. One of them said, 'Brother, I don't hate you. I love you even though I don't know who you are. You don't need to ask my forgiveness, but if you need forgiveness, I'm here to give it to you.'

"We prayed and hugged each other. And I felt this tremendous freedom and joy. I wept tears of release from the forgiveness of sin I felt—forgiveness not only from God, but also from a man, from my black brother."

Jim didn't learn until later that his friend David Tibbet was also in that stadium. He, too, heard Tony Evans's call for racial reconciliation and then watched in amazement as hundreds of men, black and white and brown, streamed to the front. He experienced some of the same emotions Fred VanderMay did as many of the white men sitting around him walked over to give him a hug, ask his forgiveness, and tell him they loved him. David says he thought, *This is the kind of unity I've been looking for all my life. This is the kind of relationship all men can have in Christ. This is a taste of what heaven will be like.*

In the meantime, Jim watched as his friend Fred, followed by Frank and Carl, finally began to make their way back through the crowd toward their seats. Then the three of them suddenly turned and headed the opposite way across the stadium. *Where in the world are they going?* Jim wondered as he hurried to follow.

When he caught up with them, Jim learned Fred and Frank had decided to seek out their younger brother, who was also in the stadium. When they found him, the brothers and their brother-in-law all talked about the racial attitudes they'd grown up with. And they vowed to begin breaking down the barriers in their lives.

Finally Jim spoke up, telling the group about his own background and pointing out how it could take just one generation to change that family heritage. Then he related the story of David Tibbet and all the other minority people who had meant so much in the life of his son.

"We Christians have a lot to learn about God's character and the unity we have in Christ," Jim concludes. "I've learned a little about that through the way God has brought together so many men and women of different colors to sustain my son's life and witness to His color blindness."

Three men. Three different stories: David, the black man who, despite wrestling all his life with issues of race and injustice, became best friends with a white brother named Mark; Jim, the white father of a severely handicapped son, who was ministered to by David and so many others of various ethnic backgrounds; and Fred, a white man struggling to know how to break through the racial barriers remaining in his life and who was challenged when Jim told how David had blessed him.

All three share the same faith in Jesus Christ, and all are responding in their own ways to the call to help break down racial barriers. Their stories are woven together tightly—a reminder, perhaps, of the way God wants all His people's lives to be intertwined.

Personal Evaluation

Do you have any friends from a different racial group? If so, how close are you? If not, why not?

In the Group

1. If you've taken a first step toward denominational reconciliation since the last session, describe it. If you haven't, when might you do so?
2. What common examples of overt and covert racism do you see in our culture?
3. What does 1 John 2:9-11 say about the nature of racism?
4. To what extent is the segregation of American churches a result of racism, and to what extent is it a matter of preferences in worship styles and musical tastes?
5. What are some strengths of other racial groups that you've come to appreciate?
6. What barriers do we need to overcome (fear, not knowing how we'll be received, etc.) to reach out across racial lines?

My Response

One individual or group that I believe God might want me to approach across a racial barrier is _____

_____

A first step I can take in the near future is _____

_____

Memory Verse

"Anyone who claims to be in the light but hates his brother is still in the darkness" (1 John 2:9).

CHAPTER 7

Introduction

Concrete has physical qualities that cause it to flow, set, and cure a certain way. Though children are given specific qualities by God, to a large degree we parents shape those qualities, helping to determine what they become—good or bad.

That child of yours is helpless in the hands of the people around him. He is pliable to their shaping; they set his mold. What will he become?

That's what Abraham Lincoln asked—who never paid more than minimum courtesy to the adults whom he passed on the street, but when he passed a child he stepped out of the way and doffed his hat. "These adults I know," he said, "but who knows what the children may become?"

These little ones, kicking in their cribs or racing about— they are tomorrow's world, our most precious possession, most powerful potential. . . .

But the awesome thing is that they receive their impressions of life from us—even their impressions of what makes godliness. . . .

Well, they are God's wonderful gift to us. Certainly they make us what we would never be if they weren't watching us and copying us!

They are the arrows of our bows, with their direction dependent upon our guidance.

They are the receivers of our batons, when we begin to tire.

They are tomorrow's heroes and rescuers and achievers— or else tomorrow's thieves and saboteurs and loafers. (Anne Ortlund, Children Are Wet Cement [Old Tappan, N.J.: Revell, 1981], pp. 38-40)

A Promise Keeper Loves and Disciplines His Children

In 1990, when 35-year-old Warren Risniak was offered the sales and marketing manager's position with a little-known computer software firm, everyone told him it would be a thankless job. People in the know warned him the company president was impossible to work for. And a lot of experts predicted the product he had to sell was going nowhere.

However, Warren's old company was restructuring. The new position promised better pay, and he did have a wife and four children under 10 to provide for. So he said, "Let's try it and see where it goes." He figured he had nothing to lose.

He was wrong on that score. But it took him almost four years to find it out.

Soon after Warren took over his new job, his company's product took off like a rocket, and he found himself on a wild and crazy ride. Sales numbers multiplied exponentially. He earned a reputation around the software industry. "Before I knew it," he says, "I was in the left-hand passing lane and couldn't get back over."

Not that he wasn't enjoying his spectacular success. He got immense ego satisfaction from his work. While it was gratifying to be respected, it proved even headier stuff to be needed. The phones would be ringing, the fax spewing out paper, his office crowded with assistants wanting immediate answers, other people lined up outside his door, and a crack sales staff of 25 awaiting his instructions. "I was eating it up," Warren says. "Some days I remember thinking, *Man, I don't care if I ever go home again.*"

One reason he may have thought that way was that, despite all his exciting success at work (and to large degree because of it), things weren't going well at home. Warren and Bonnie Risniak had known when he took the job that it would be time consuming. What they hadn't anticipated was how it would become *all* consuming.

> **"The job took so much out of me," Warren confesses, "that I had nothing left to give to my family when I came home."**

"The job took so much out of me," Warren confesses, "that I had nothing left to give to my family when I came home."

Travel created a big part of the problem. Warren would often be gone two or two and a half weeks a month. A lot of his trips were to the Far East—Taiwan, Japan, Hong Kong—and he would need almost a week to recover from the jet lag. He routinely made one-day trips to California, arriving back in Charlotte, North Carolina, at daybreak and heading into the office by midmorning. So even when he was home, he was so physically and emotionally drained that he wasn't ready to shoulder any of the load Bonnie carried by herself in his absence. Thus, she often felt more alone after Warren returned than she did when he was halfway around the world.

"Warren would bring home all these international newspapers with his picture in them—at a business conference, sometimes signing a contract, other times handing out or receiving some industry award. Big PR stuff. I'd see those pictures and think, *That's my husband!* But I couldn't identify at all with what he was doing. While he was jetting all over the world, I was home alone with four kids driving car pool, wiping runny noses, and changing messy diapers. Warren and I seemed to be living two completely different lifestyles."

That created an even bigger challenge than most couples face in working out their individual roles and mutual expectations. For a long time, Warren assured himself everything would be fine at home because Bonnie was strong and amazingly resourceful. She not only cared for the kids, but she also managed the household and all the other routine family affairs—getting the lawn mowed, the cars serviced, the bills paid. All that achievement gave her a sense of independence and fulfillment.

What she wasn't getting was any sense of support. Bonnie survived the week by thinking, *When Warren gets back this weekend, he'll step in and save me, take over with the kids, and do all this stuff I didn't get to.* But the superhero role never quite fit Warren. And even when the Risniaks decided they could afford to pay someone to do things around the house so he'd have time for the family, that never seemed enough, either.

It wasn't that Warren didn't love his family anymore or didn't want to be there for Bonnie and the kids. He did. But shifting gears from work to home got harder and harder.

Making matters worse was what the Risniaks call the "room service mind-set" Warren got when he traveled. He worked hard hours on the road, but his clothes were laundered for him. His meals were prepared at his bidding. The people hosting him looked after his needs. He only had to talk to people when he called on them.

"You develop habits," Warren says. "Some are very lazy or at least narcissistic when you travel. There are all these people whose job it is to serve you. And there's always time in your room alone when no one is bothering you or expecting anything. Then you come home and it's like whiplash—'Whee! Let's go! Can you do that? What about this?' I wanted to scream, 'Wait a minute! Where's room service?'"

And Bonnie would be ready for a little room service herself—or at least a dinner out. But Warren, tired of restaurant meals, was always ready for home cooking.

Another area where the Risniaks' expectations came into conflict was in their parenting roles. Because Warren didn't spend much time with the kids, the time he did spend he wanted to be fun. So he'd be a big "playmate" and leave the tougher job of discipline up to Bonnie. "I hated always being the one to play the bad guy," she says. "I desperately wanted help in this area, but I just didn't get it."

Looking back, Warren says he should have recognized the growing problems. He feels the Lord was trying to get through to him the whole time. "But I ignored the problems. I told myself, *Bonnie's doing a great job with the kids. I know it's hard, but she's terrific. She always rises to the occasion. It's fulfilling her and making her a stronger person.* And it was.

"I also told myself, *I'm just doing what I have to do to earn a living for my family.* Like a lot of men, I had a tremendous ability to ignore problems by trying to rationalize them away."

But at some level, Warren did recognize a problem. And in an attempt to balance family and work, he put in a fax line at home. He figured he'd be able to come home earlier—by 7:00 or 8:00 most nights. But then about 9:30 every evening, the faxes would begin arriving from all over the world. And they'd continue till midnight or 1:00 in the morning. "When I allowed work into my home through that door," Warren says, "it kicked the rest of the doors in, and I could find no refuge. Home was just another place to go to work."

In an attempt to get Warren to spend more time with their children, Bonnie encouraged him to take an active role in their church's AWANA program, a Christian kids' club ministry. In part because of her pressure, but also because he recognized the same need, Warren agreed to take charge of the group games and activities. He figured the responsibility would force him to get out of the office one night a week.

While the strategy worked as planned, it also created added stress—at work and at home. "Things never settled down at our office until at least 7:00 or 7:30," Warren says. "So when I started leaving at 5:00 on Wednesday, colleagues were always asking, 'Where are you going?' or at least pointedly looking at their watches as I walked past their offices. That made leaving very hard, because I wanted to be seen as a team player; I wanted everyone to know I was pulling my weight. I knew it irritated other people when I left and they couldn't. That embarrassed and frustrated me. So I'd be upset and irritable all the way home."

When he did get home, always at least a few minutes later than he'd planned, the entire family and half the kids in the neighborhood would be out in the driveway, waiting impatiently. Bonnie would hand him a plate of food, and he'd slide into the passenger seat of the family Suburban, balancing dinner on his lap while his wife tried to make up time in rush-hour traffic. More than once, she had to hit the brakes, and Warren's supper ended up on the floor. "I'd be zigzagging in and out of traffic," Bonnie recalls, "kids would be singing AWANA songs in the back, and Warren and I would be silently seething in our seats, refusing to talk to each other—all in the name of ministry to our kids."

When they got to church, Warren admits he wasn't the most patient of group leaders. He'd often grow upset and snap at any kids who didn't respond immediately to his instructions.

The same kind of irritability often cropped up at home in regard to discipline. He'd be in his withdrawal mode when the kids would start acting up. And either Bonnie would finally ask him to intervene, or the incident would progress to the point he could no longer ignore it. Either way, he'd be angry at being forced into action and would respond by lashing out at the kids.

Warren admits he's always had a problem dealing with anger. He's the kind of person Bonnie calls a "stuffer." He stuffs his feelings beneath the surface for as long as he can, sometimes bearing a grudge for days, before something—often totally unrelated—triggers an explosion.

"As the stress continued to build, it seemed I was angry about something all the time," Warren says. "I'd blow up at Bonnie or one of the kids. I'd get furious if someone cut me off in traffic. I'd get angry when I couldn't find my Bible because someone had moved it."

Warren Risniak didn't like the person he was becoming. He didn't feel good about the kind of husband he was to Bonnie or the kind of father he was to their children. And as time went on, he decided he didn't particularly like his job anymore, either. The pace never slowed; the demands never ceased. And if the work itself didn't create enough stress, his boss made things even worse. The owner of the company, the man Warren reported to, managed by intimidation. He was never satisfied, never offered a word of encouragement. "I got to where I wasn't sleeping because I was having nightmares," Warren says. "I had stomach problems. I actually hated my job. But I didn't know where else to get the self-worth I was getting there."

He finally reached the point of burnout. "My whole perspective changed. Instead of looking forward to Monday mornings with a plan for attacking the week, I was on the defensive, not wanting to have to act. I got so numb I didn't care anymore. And when you don't care about something you were getting a lot of gratification from, it becomes like an unrequited lover. This thing that was feeding you is not feeding you. You're getting nothing back.

"That made me angry and bitter and even melancholy at times. I experienced great mood swings. It was total emotional disorientation. I lost my moorings. I flailed and struggled to find something to replace what I'd lost.

"I should have known better. I'd been a Christian for more than 10 years. I went to a strong, Bible-believing church. I knew all the things I should have been doing. But I still allowed myself to slide spiritually."

By the summer of 1993, Bonnie Risniak had also reached the point of burnout with Warren's job—and with Warren. She was the one who suggested he go to the Promise Keepers conference in Boulder. "You have the frequent flier miles," she told him.

So Warren went—loaded with emotional baggage but desperately searching for relief. Two of the speakers really hit home with him. First was Dr. Howard Hendricks's talk on the need for mentoring relationships. "I knew I needed that kind of accountability before I could make any changes," Warren says. And then there was Dr. James Dobson's talk about what wives wanted him to say to the men at Promise Keepers. Dobson challenged Warren and 50,000 other men to become the spiritual leaders of their homes. Warren remembers, "He spoke about achievement and awards and how, in the end, none of those would matter. How all we could take into eternity with us would be our family and our loved ones. That really hit me, too."

The first thing Warren did when he got home was to ask an older man he respected in his church to be a mentor to him. "I knew I needed a normalization of my life," he says. "My life had gotten so far out of balance, my wife couldn't counterbalance me. I needed a man who could hit me square between the eyes and make me accountable. And I wanted an older man who would have the advantage of age over me so I'd be more inclined to listen to him." But he also sought out a man about his own age to act as a Barnabas—someone who could relate to his life experience and still level with him.

Deciding what he should do and actually doing it were two different things.

In honestly sharing his struggle with these men, it wasn't long until Warren decided the only hope for restoring the balance to his life—the only way to be the kind of husband and father he wanted to be—was to give up his job. But deciding what he should do and actually doing it were two different things. "I didn't want to quit," he says, "before I found something else that would pay me the same amount of money."

That reluctance to take corrective action only increased the stress, however, for Bonnie as well as Warren. "He told me all about these insights he'd gotten at Promise Keepers," she says, "how family needed to be a higher priority than his work. Yet he kept right on going to the same job and the same pressures every day. And I'd think, *Why tell me what you need to do and then not care enough to do it?* My feelings were hurt by that."

For almost a year, Warren waited, looking for and planning a way out. Time with his mentor and his accountability partner slowly reinforced his resolve. A family-life conference he and Bonnie attended further convicted him about the kind of father he needed to be. What it came down to was a matter of obedience—and faith.

He agonized over his decision right up to the time he finally turned in his resignation. But he had lunch that day with his Barnabas, who told him, "Just do it." And he did.

The parting from his company turned out to be more amicable than Warren had imagined possible. His boss offered him a consultant role to maintain the account of the firm's biggest client. And that deal became the foundation on which Warren began to build his own business. After the better part of a year on his own, Warren has nowhere near the income he was making before. But, he says, "God has provided all we've needed. And when I look back at all those months of agonizing over my decision to quit, I can't for the life of me figure out what I was so worried about. I think, *What was the big problem?* Because even after the initial sense of relief and euphoria wore off, I've never doubted I did the right thing."

Relatives and friends noticed a difference in Warren right away. "It's like you're a different person," they told him. And he worked to reinforce that change by making himself accountable to a group of men from his church who went with him to his second Promise Keepers in Indianapolis in 1994. Reading and talking with Bonnie also gave him new perspectives to help the transformation process.

Warren says he found that *The Hidden Value of a Man,* by Gary Smalley and Dr. John Trent, offered valuable insights into his own fathering habits—particularly their comparison of a man's authority to two different kinds of swords. In the world, a man needs to be forceful and swing a big, silver sword to make his way and attain his goals. But the close relationships of home and family demand a defter, gentler touch—more like a delicate, golden dagger. "That analogy really made the point for me," Warren says. "I immediately saw how I'd too often come charging home swinging the big, silver sword of authority I used as a boss at work. I'd interact with Bonnie and the kids the same way I would deal with my work—being forceful, decisive, sometimes adversarial, and often an authoritarian leader instead of trying to be sensitive, understanding, and responsive."

Bonnie could appreciate that analogy as well. "Warren always assumed I was as tough as he was," she says, "but I wasn't. His silver-sword approach at home caused a lot of wounds, not just with me, but with our three sensitive daughters, too." Now that he's not so consumed by the battle for survival at work, Warren says it's a lot easier to set aside that silver sword and have kinder relationships with his family.

Indeed, Bonnie sees a real change in Warren's fathering. The simple fact that he's home more keeps him much more in touch. But he's also making a deliberate attempt to involve himself in his kids' lives. "There were some years there when I'm not sure he knew there was such a thing as homework," Bonnie says with a laugh. "Now he actually knows the names of their teachers. Most days he not only drives our youngest daughter to preschool, but he even walks her in and helps her get settled."

The entire family sits down together for breakfast and supper almost every day. Warren says that, too, helps him better connect as a father, which in turn makes it much easier to be the spiritual leader of his family. "When we have family devotions now," he says, "I can help my kids see how to apply biblical truths, because I have an understanding of their lives. If we're reading a passage about kindness to others, I can suggest five-year-old Mandy could apply that by making a point to be friendly to the new girl who started at her school yesterday. I'm plugged in to the kids' lives enough to know and do that."

The kids feel involved with their dad as well. They all get a kick out of stuffing envelopes and helping send out his business mailings. To recognize their help, Warren got all of them their own business cards. He's also written each child a long letter to be opened on their 16th birthdays—a declaration of his love and appreciation for them as individuals, a sharing of his hopes and dreams for them, and an offering of wisdom and advice. ("Just in case I'm not around when they reach 16," he says.) The kids all know about the letters and can't wait to open them. The oldest, Hope, is the envy of her siblings because she's got only two years to go.

According to Bonnie, all the kids are happier and doing better in school than ever before. And she feels the transformation in Warren's life has come just in time. Their son, who is fast approaching adolescence, has begun showing some of the same patterns of anger that Warren struggled with for so long. "So I'm beginning to teach him the lessons I'm learning about dealing with anger in a healthy manner," Warren says.

"And then," Bonnie adds, "there's our oldest daughter, who's already convinced me that it takes two parents to handle a teenager. Some days I'm not sure 10 parents would be enough. I don't know how I'd survive the next few years without Warren's new level of involvement."

But Bonnie isn't the only one in the Risniak family to recognize and appreciate the difference in Warren—as evidenced by 12-year-old Taylor's Father's Day gift last year. "He gave me a beautiful painting he'd done for me—of two swords," Warren says. "A big, silver one and a smaller, more delicate and beautiful gold one. I had the picture framed to hang in my office as a constant reminder of the kind of father I want to be."

Personal Evaluation

When your work becomes too consuming, what costs do you pay? What price do your children pay?

To what extent do you feel the hours you work are under your control? If you think you have no choice but to work long hours in your current job, how can you make sure your kids still feel loved?

In the Group

1. What step toward racial reconciliation have you thought of taking? Have you done that yet? If so, what happened? If not, when might you?

2. Warren Risniak stated that he, like most men, has a great ability to ignore problems. Why do we tend to do that? What happens when we do?

3. To what extent do peer pressure and the drive for success at work keep you away from home more than you would like?

4. If an objective observer looked at how you use your time and money, how important would he conclude your children are to you? Why?

5. What can a noncustodial dad do to have a better relationship with his kids?

6. If you were to set aside one night a week just to do things with your family, how do you think they would react? Why?

7. To whom have you given permission to hold you accountable for the job you're doing as a father? If the answer is no one, to whom will you give this authority?

8. Psalm 127:4 says children are "like arrows in the hands of a warrior." What does that mean for us as fathers today?

My Response

Complete the following prayer, and then say it to God: "Heavenly Father, because I realize how important my children are, with Your help I'll work at being a better father this next week by _____

_____ "

Memory Verse

"Sons are a heritage from the LORD, children a reward from him" (Ps. 127:3).

CHAPTER 8

Introduction

If a man wants to experience the power and grace of God, if he wants to see the Holy Spirit work, there is no more powerful arena for this than in his sexual life.

Our sexuality hits the very core of who we are. Much of the validation that women get in friendships, men get from the sexual relationship. Much of our identity and ego is at stake. If you watch TV, it appears that our culture evaluates us by how well we do in this area. The message: As goes our sexual success, so goes everything else.

We men have an incredible ability—a disability, really—to disassociate one area of our lives from another and justify wrong behavior that we would find unacceptable in others. The classic recent example is Aldrich Ames, the CIA employee who sold many U.S. secrets to the former Soviet Union. He was betraying his country on the one hand, yet he was working for his country on the other. In the same way, one survey found that more than 50 percent of the men who attend Promise Keepers conferences have a personal problem with pornographic thoughts. Some are fighting it, but some really aren't.

Yet in 1 Corinthians 6:18-20, God (through the apostle Paul) calls us to a higher standard. We're to honor Him with our bodies because they are a temple of the Holy Spirit, bought at the price of His own Son. In 1 Thessalonians 4:3-8, we're commanded to avoid sexual immorality, and then the passage closes with, "Therefore, he who rejects this instruction does not reject man but God, who gives you his Holy Spirit" (v. 8).

That's a high standard, indeed. And many Christian men, like Kurt Stansell, struggle with it daily. We expect that many of you reading this will identify with his story, at least in part. We know that the God who is giving him victory can and wants to do the same for you.

A Promise Keeper Protects His Sexual Purity

By his own admission, Kurt Stansell is a sex addict.

Kurt is also one of those men most acquaintances look at as someone who "has it all." Married for 13 years to a wonderful wife, he's the father of an eight-year-old son and a three-year-old daughter. Soon after he turned 30, Kurt and a friend both left promising careers with a major bank to start what has become, in five years, their own successful investment counseling business. Kurt's also one of the founding elders of his church, which is among the fastest-growing evangelical congregations in the Bay Area of California. His pastors and fellow lay leaders all praise his spiritual leadership. One of them even went so far as to call him "an awesome man of God" who has been and is being used in a mighty way by the Lord.

Kurt Stansell is one of the last people anyone who knew him would have suspected of having a problem with sexual addiction. (We refer to it as an addiction because as you'll see, it's powerful, it's cyclical in nature, and it leads progressively downward.) But he did. And he does.

"I grew up in a strong Christian home," Kurt says. "My dad was a military chaplain, so we moved a lot, and I spent several years of my youth in Europe and the Far East. My parents were committed, godly people who devoted themselves to a ministry with American military personnel. They also raised me and my younger brother and sister with a clear understand-

ing of the gospel. I've had a personal relationship with Christ from the time
I was a preschooler. Bible teaching and Scripture memorization were regular
parts of my upbringing. I had what I always considered a wonderful, almost
perfect, childhood."

During his early teenage years, Kurt developed a natural curiosity about
sexual matters. He regularly read Dr. Joyce Brothers's question-and-answer
column in Good Housekeeping, and his mom gave him a couple of Christian
books that covered the basic facts of life. But for some reason, Kurt says, "My
dad wasn't there for me at that point." So Kurt had a lot of questions he didn't
know how to get answered.

Occasionally he'd risk talking to one of the young Christian servicemen
who were in and out of his home. Kurt developed enough of a relationship
with one married guy to ask a specific question. The soldier answered honestly
and then discussed some of the temptations he'd experienced as a teenager.
He even talked in an accepting and frank manner about masturbation, something Kurt knew about but had never done.

Within a few days of that discussion, Kurt says, "I had my first experience
with masturbation. Afterward I felt very ashamed. At the same time, I
couldn't help remembering how exciting the physical sensation had been. So
I felt confused by the mixed emotional reaction and had no one I felt I could
talk to about that, either."

Masturbation soon became a regular habit. "I think I had about as strong
a relationship with God as a 15- or 16-year-old kid can have," Kurt says, "and
I really wanted to know: Was this right or was it wrong?"

He never did get a straight, clear answer to that question. The Christian
books he read offered differing opinions. And the speakers who talked about
sex at a Christian youth camp he attended avoided the subject.

When he was 17 and visiting friends at a missionary school not far from
the base where his family lived in the Philippines, Kurt was challenged by a
chapel speaker who talked about purity, commitment, and following God.
Kurt rededicated his life at the close of that service.

Later that day, he spotted that speaker walking down a campus sidewalk
alone. Kurt hurried to catch up and asked if he could talk to the man for a
minute. "Then I told him about the commitment I'd made in response to his
challenge that morning, and in an awkward, roundabout way, I let him know
I was struggling with masturbation. I think I felt that if I'd just confess my

problem to someone and have him pray for me, I'd find extra strength the next time I was tempted."

Indeed, that's what seemed to happen. The speaker listened and encouraged Kurt to be sensitive to what he felt God was saying to him. He prayed for him and tried to encourage him by advising, "This is something you're going to have to deal with day to day. And you'll need to rely on God's strength."

"That was a very positive experience for me," Kurt says. "From it I found a sense of victory that lasted for several months."

Kurt's downfall came with his initial exposure to pornography.

His downfall came with his initial exposure to pornography. "It was a casual, almost accidental thing at first," he says. "I was walking along the streets of Manila when I passed a newsstand overflowing with pornographic magazines. Unlike most displays in the U.S., where only the magazine logo is displayed, everything was out in the open—plastered all over. I didn't stop to look that day. But after that, every time I walked past a newsstand, I'd slow my pace ever so slightly and cast a few furtive glances at the covers of those magazines. Just that bit of exposure proved enough to fuel my adolescent fantasies and more guilt."

Coming back to the States to college provided a relief from Kurt's growing sexual temptations. The conservative Christian college he attended on the West Coast served as a natural shelter from the kind of material he had been seeing every day in the Philippines. There was strong Christian fellowship with roommates and other friends. And starting his junior year, there was also Martha, a sophomore girl Kurt soon became serious about.

"Although we both had strong commitments to remaining virgins until marriage, we gradually developed a fairly physical relationship," Kurt says. That helped to reduce his nascent fascination with pornography, but it only fueled his growing sexual addiction. And Kurt admits, "Each week when I drove into the city to tutor a Vietnamese kid, I'd go right by an X-rated theater. I always read the titles of the films on the marquee, and I was curious about what kind of stuff they showed. But I never stopped and went in."

By the time Kurt graduated from college, he and Martha were engaged and planned to be married the following year when she finished college. In the meantime, he took some time off to travel, visiting the missionary family of one of his college roommates in Brazil for several weeks. He concluded his trip with a week alone in Rio de Janeiro.

While there, Kurt discovered an X-rated theater just a couple blocks down from his hotel. "I walked right by it several times in my comings and goings," he says, "and each time the temptation to stop and go in grew a little stronger. Finally, it just seemed too easy to cough up the dollar or so it cost to walk in. I was surprised at how many people were inside. It was fairly full. There were actually couples there on dates."

Feeling terribly embarrassed even though he was in a city of 14 million strangers, he didn't want anyone to see him, so he quickly slipped into the back of the darkened theater and sat down. "I guess I'd been pretty naive about pornography up to that point," Kurt says. "The usual newsstand magazines were about as much as I'd ever looked through. I couldn't believe what the movie showed. I watched with equal parts fascination and disgust, experiencing both arousal and abhorrence.

"Before the movie ended, I slipped out of the theater with a tremendous sense of self-loathing. *You've really hit rock bottom now,* I told myself. *This is the most disgusting thing you've ever done. You can never tell anyone you could have been tempted by, let alone gone in and watched, a movie like that.*"

Kurt went back to his room, got down on his knees, asked God to forgive him, and promised never to do anything like that again. And when he got back to the States and began anticipating his upcoming wedding, he thought, *Marriage will be terrific. That'll be the end of this kind of temptation. I'll have a legitimate sexual release. That'll be the solution.* Unfortunately, it wasn't.

Shortly after the wedding, Kurt landed an entry-level job at a banking company, and he and Martha moved to Atlanta. He had a number of training sessions at hotels near the airport, and he noticed that most of the city's topless clubs were also in that part of town. "As I drove by this one place every day for a week," he says, "it seemed to pull me like a magnet: *I wonder what goes on in there?* Finally one day when our training let out early, I stopped and made a pretense of going in to use the club's rest room. I was both relieved and disappointed that nothing seemed to be happening in the middle of the afternoon.

"I wondered, *When does it start?* Then I told myself, *You idiot! You shouldn't even be in here! What were you thinking!* And I hurried out feeling guilty once more."

Not long after that, Kurt went to Boston for a two-day training conference. He stayed overnight in a hotel near downtown. "It was the first time I had ever stayed alone in a hotel with cable," he says. "It was so easy to turn on the TV, flip to the adult-film channel, and watch a full-length movie. It wasn't real hard-core, but it was definitely pornography. I sat there and watched the whole thing that night right after dinner."

Then he went out for a walk. On a corner just a few blocks from his hotel, two men stopped him and asked, "You need coke?"

"No, no," Kurt said, backing away.

"You need a girl?" they asked.

"No," he said again.

"You need a guy?"

"No, thank you, I'm fine," he said as he turned and walked away quickly.

"There was obviously all kinds of stuff going on along that strip," Kurt continues, "which may be why it didn't seem like such a big deal to step into the third or fourth club I came to with a 'XXXGirls, Girls, GirlsXXX' sign out front. But when I walked through the door, it seemed everyone in the joint turned and looked at me. I felt so obviously out of place, I backed right out onto the sidewalk, hurried down the street to my hotel, and watched another movie on TV.

"I went home from Boston feeling like a real jerk and thinking that if Martha knew what I'd done, what I'd been tempted to do, she'd be devastated. It was as if I'd betrayed her and she wouldn't love me anymore if she knew I had this problem. I promised myself and God—once again—that I wouldn't do those things anymore."

But there were just so many temptations. One Saturday afternoon while he waited for his car to be serviced a few miles from his apartment, Kurt walked down the street, and there was an adult bookstore. Whenever he went to the airport, there were always the magazine stands. And it seemed that everywhere he went in the city, he'd see signs advertising adult entertainment clubs.

Then his company sent Kurt to an intensive six-week training session in Chicago. His hotel was only a couple blocks from the city's famous Rush Street district. Martha wasn't with him. So he started thinking, *This is my big chance to finally find out what's going on with adult entertainment.*

Kurt describes the experience. "I walked over to Rush Street, went into the first club I came to, and sat down at a table. The place had a two-drink minimum, so I ordered a beer. I don't even drink! But I sat there all by myself, sipping my brew and watching the girls doing their thing on stage.

"The adrenaline rush I experienced watching those dancers was significant. Everything up to that point had been two-dimensional—on the printed page or on a screen—and had seemed almost artificial. Here were real, live women—literally in the flesh. And yet there seemed to be something safely impersonal and anonymous about the experience. When I walked out of that bar, I sensed every nerve in my body was alive. But so was my conscience. I felt so incredibly guilty as I walked back to my hotel that I said to myself, *Well, now you've done that. That's as low as you're going to go. You're never going to do anything like that again.*

"And for a long time, I didn't. Yet the seed was planted. Another barrier was down."

While it was some time before Kurt felt tempted to return to a live club, printed pornography continued to entice him. Back home in Atlanta, when he'd stop for gas at a convenience mart, he would sometimes pause for a few minutes at the magazine rack and flip through men's magazines. "I felt pretty anonymous in a city where we still didn't know many people," Kurt explains. "Martha and I had started going to a church and had become good friends with one other couple. But in terms of getting caught, of having someone spot me and being embarrassed, I felt pretty immune."

Weeks and even months would go by when he thought he was doing fine—reading the Bible and praying regularly. But then the temptation would strike again, and for a week or two he would struggle with it, driving by the same place and telling himself, *No, you're not going to stop and go in there.* And then he would.

"In a way, it was almost satisfying when I finally gave in," Kurt says. "It was like there was this big struggle and all this tension building up as I wrestled with the temptation. And yet afterward there was a tremendous sense of relief and release. It was done. It was over. There was no more tension and no more temptation—for a while. I'd tell myself, *That's it. Never again. There's no reason to go back.*"

After every incident, Kurt would feel a need to be especially attentive to Martha in an attempt to ease his guilt and make up for what he'd done. That became such a part of the pattern that he began to rationalize, *This could actu-*

ally be good for our relationship. I'm putting less pressure on Martha to meet my sexual needs. His sexual endurance would be better for a day or two after he had masturbated, meaning less tendency toward premature ejaculation, so he would tell himself, *This is better for Martha, too.*

"Sometimes I could almost see my episodes with pornography as God-given escapes that I needed," Kurt says. "It became easier and easier to turn off the rational part of my brain and justify the behavior. Yet I think I always knew deep down that I was deluding myself, because even when the guilt began to fade, there was always this sense of emptiness and disappointment afterward."

The pattern continued for years. At home in Atlanta, there were periodic stops at convenience-store magazine racks, an occasional X-rated video rental when he knew Martha wasn't going to be home, and excuses made during shopping trips together so he could slip into a bookstore by himself. Visits to live entertainment clubs were reserved for out-of-town business trips.

> **Personal evaluation:** Have you ever found yourself planning or participating in the types of activities Kurt mentions? If so, how did it make you feel?

The Stansells moved to San Jose, California, when Kurt got a big promotion. They soon got into an exciting new church, where Kurt joined a weekly men's prayer breakfast and he and Martha eagerly joined a care group of couples their ages. "I really felt a desperate need for fellowship," Kurt admits. Another guy asked him to team teach a Sunday school class, and Kurt's strong Bible background got him selected to help lead yet another care group. He and a fellow who had been in both groups also agreed to have an accountability relationship, and they began getting together one on one every week.

"I really liked Stan," Kurt says. "He was a terrific Christian guy—someone I thought I could relate to and be honest with. Not that I was very honest with him in the beginning. I'd tell myself, *As soon as I get my act together with this pornography business, I'm going to have 100 percent accountability with Stan. There's no way I can share where I've been; it's just too shameful. He'd never be able to accept me.*"

The two men started meeting for breakfast every week, and Kurt used a lot of euphemisms to avoid getting too specific. "Well, I really screwed up this week. I saw something I shouldn't have," he'd say. "But I think we both knew

I was talking about masturbation," he says now.

Despite the limited openness, Kurt's relationship with Stan was positive and encouraging. They challenged each other to be better Christian men, better husbands, and better fathers. Yet the sexual sins continued.

In Kurt's words, "I was like a plane that's gone into a nosedive—heading down, down, down. My meetings with Stan were like when the pilot pulls up on the stick yet feels this tremendous G-force pulling him down harder even after he begins to come out of the dive. The momentum is still there, dragging him down. That's kind of where I was. I was making the right moves with this accountability business, but there was such a momentum in my life—the denial, the impaired thinking, the rationalization. All the patterns of temptation, all the trigger points, were still there."

On his next business trip, after a week alone in Houston, he began to feel the urge. He picked up the phone book to find where the topless entertainment was, then drove to the nearest place. "The club was real classy," he says, "not at all seedy like the other places I'd been. I went in and watched the dancers for a while. I noticed the girls were giving personal attention to some of the men."

When one of the girls offered to dance for Kurt, he said yes. When she finished, she told him the fee was $40. "Suddenly the whole thing changed," Kurt says. "The bubble burst; the fantasy was gone. One minute her attitude had been 'Let me please you. You're wonderful'—that kind of stuff. The next minute it was 'Where's my money?' By the time I got out of there, the image was shattered. It was painfully obvious that I had been used and that I had used her—we both knew it. I was so disgusted with myself."

Back in his hotel room, he thought, *Now you've really hit bottom.* He had never interacted with a person before. "To top it off," he says, "on this same trip to Houston, there had been a very attractive girl in the training class with me. I'd talked to her during breaks, and we had lunch together a couple times. I actually witnessed to her. But by the end of that week, I went home thinking, *You're not invulnerable to an affair. If you'd been in Houston another two weeks at the rate you were going, you could have really messed up.*"

That thought scared him enough that he determined to make his accountability work by being honest with Stan. He still didn't divulge everything, but he told Stan more than he had before. Then Kurt learned that a man who had played a major role in his spiritual development had been accused of sexual misconduct and had seen his ministry come to an end. "That news was the straw that broke the camel's back for me," Kurt says. "That was what said to me, 'Kurt, you are going down in flames unless you can be 100 percent honest.' "

He also thought, *Someday you're going to get caught, and it would be really good if you had at least one person who could testify that you went kicking and screaming, that you were fighting against this addiction.*

One night when their families had gotten together, Kurt and Stan went for a walk. Out on the street, Kurt asked, "Stan, what's the worst thing you've ever done in your whole life?"

Stan described a sexual experience he had years before. "I could see it was hard for him to tell me; it was something that still haunted him," Kurt says. "He worried, 'What if a child was born?' He said he had this recurring nightmare of a kid coming back and saying, 'Hey, Dad.' "

Hearing Stan's story made Kurt want to tell his. But Stan's incident had happened a long time ago, back when he was still a young, single man. Kurt's story was painfully fresh, going on every day even though he was an elder in the church. "I nearly choked on the words," Kurt says, "but I got them out. Stan listened. He didn't condemn me. We prayed for each other."

> **Personal evaluation:** Do you have someone other than your wife with whom you can share your secret temptations and failures? If so, how has that helped? If not, where might you find such a person?

After praying with Stan, Kurt noticed an immediate difference. "The temptation I faced was cut in half," he explains. "Not that I didn't mess up again. I did. But often when I knew I was going to be on a business trip, or when I felt the temptation building, I'd tell Stan or just think about having to tell him if I gave in, and there truly was less of a temptation."

Kurt still wrestled with questions like why a secular friend could go to a bachelor party, watch a hired stripper, and then go on with life without seeming to give the experience a second thought. Yet Kurt would struggle for weeks with the temptation to go into a topless club and then wallow in guilt for just as long after he gave in. Even when he fought off the temptation, it was a huge struggle. Why did this addiction have so much power over him?

"As I prayed and studied and pondered those questions, and as I honestly talked about the issue with Stan," Kurt says, "I began to understand what shame does. When we Christians try to hide something in the darkness, we give Satan incredible license to work in our lives. It's like handing power tools over to him and saying, 'Here, do what you will in my life,' because he's got free rein with all that's hidden when God's light is not shining on it. So I learned that the more open I could be, the less of a hold Satan seemed to have."

That insight was part of Kurt's motivation in deciding to tell his pastor, "I don't think I should continue my role in the leadership of our church. Not while I'm struggling so in my own personal life. I'm dealing with some major flaws."

"Well, do you want to tell me about them?" the pastor asked.

"I hadn't planned on telling him everything," Kurt says, "but once I got started, I just spilled my guts. When I finished, he looked at me and said, 'You might want to think about a more public confession.' I swallowed and thought, *I don't know if I'm open to that. I'm not sure that standing up in front of the church on Sunday morning is the most appropriate step for me to take.*"

Seeing Kurt's hesitation, the pastor assured him, "Maybe it should be in a men's group, a small-group Bible study of guys or something like that. You're going to be part of the group going to the Promise Keepers conference next month; perhaps some opportunity will arise for sharing there."

Kurt told his pastor he would think about it. And as he did, he realized that each step toward openness so far had reduced his temptation—first with Stan, then with his pastor. But to tell anyone else? He just wasn't sure about exposing his darkest secrets to more light.

On the final night of the conference, however, Kurt came to the realization that a lot of other men were probably struggling, too—if not with sexual addiction, then with secrets of their own. And he became convicted that he needed to tell his story to some other guys he could trust, not so much to make a public confession but to ask for their support and even encourage them to admit their own needs. That night, Kurt stayed up late and wrote out a brief summary of his story.

The next morning, when some of his friends from church gathered for breakfast, as they began saying how God had spoken to them through the conference, Kurt made his confession. And his friends did, indeed, offer acceptance and a promise of their prayer support. Most admitted needs of their own.

After talking at length with Stan, his pastor, and now some of his friends at Promise Keepers, Kurt felt the last step he needed to take toward openness and freedom was to be honest with Martha. She held the keys to release the last of his chains. He needed her acceptance and forgiveness most of all to destroy the cycle of sin, self-loathing, and shame.

He knew he needed to proceed prayerfully and cautiously, however. Before Promise Keepers, when he had talked to his pastor the first time, Kurt had stated that one of his goals was to confess to Martha. The pastor had recommended care on that score. He'd warned Kurt to make sure that whatever was said would be productive and necessary without creating needless torment for Martha. He recounted the experience of one of his counselees in being too detailed in his description of incidents, scenes, the women involved, and his own reactions. "That kind of play-by-play description was very difficult for the man's wife," the pastor said. "And I don't think being that vivid helped either of them. You can be honest and clear about what you did without going into a lot of detail about the sin."

Kurt was so uptight about confessing to Martha that he remembers the anxiety surrounding their first conversation far better than he does the details. But everything about that talk sticks in Martha's mind as if it were yesterday. "We were visiting at my folks' house," she says, "sleeping on a mattress on the floor in their den. It was well past midnight, and we'd had such a busy day that all I wanted to do was sleep. But as soon as we lay down, I could tell Kurt really wanted to talk. And I could tell from his eyes that it was something very important. That's when he told me he'd made a confession at Promise Keepers to some men from our church. And then he repeated, pretty much word for word, what he'd said to them.

"All I could do was listen—in stunned shock. I'd never imagined anything like that. Kurt was obviously trying to be real sensitive and gentle in telling me. But there's just no good way to hear something like that from your husband. At least he wasn't at all defensive. His primary tone was apologetic and remorseful. I remember he said, 'I'm really afraid that what I've been doing has affected the way you feel about yourself, and I feel really bad about that.' He asked me to please forgive him, and he said he desperately hoped I could still love him and that he was telling me this not because he wanted to hurt me, but because he wanted to change and have a better relationship with me from now on."

As the initial shock wore off, however, it did hurt her—horribly. And after the hurt settled in, she also felt sadness and anger.

Kurt remembers Martha seemed painfully quiet, and they didn't talk much that first night. It wasn't until one night a short time later, as they got ready for bed, that she told him that ever since he'd confessed, she'd been unable to stop thinking about a scene she'd watched in the movie *The Graduate*. The Dustin Hoffman character had taken his girlfriend into some topless entertainment place, and the girl had been devastated. Martha began to cry as she told Kurt, "It really haunts me to think that you walked into places like that and were part of scenes like that."

Part of Kurt wanted to run from his wife's pain and not have to deal with it. But instead he told her, "I see four things going on here that we need to keep in mind as we work through this together. Maybe it helps to see them as four corners of a page.

"Number one, I'm really sorry. I feel this huge guilt because I've really betrayed you. I feel like I'm on my hands and knees, coming to you and begging you to take me back and allow me to prove myself to you again.

"In an opposite corner, I want to say, 'Hey, look, there's lots of guys out there who are a whole lot worse than me. They're not trying to be honest; they don't even struggle. They've had affairs, and they're not apologetic for whatever reason. I'm putting a whole lot of effort in here, and I hope you appreciate it.'

"Then on the third corner of the page, I really need to experience your love and acceptance and forgiveness. That's a huge part of what I need to get past this cycle of shame, and that's one of the reasons I've told you. Because when I feel your love, it breaks the bond. It makes me realize how grateful I am and how I don't want to betray you anymore.

"And the final corner is kind of where we're at right now. I really need to hear and be a part of your pain and your regret—as much as I hate to hear it. So I want you to know that you can share as much of that as you need to. I realize you need to express your pain if you're going to work through it, and I need to hear it because it's part of my reality therapy. It helps me see what was really going on. It brings home the truth of my betrayal; it breaks the fantasy; it's not a victimless crime. I'm painfully aware of who the victim is and what it's done to our relationship. And it really begins to destroy the temptation when I can see my behavior for what it is.

"So those are the four things going on, and we may be at different areas on that page at different times, but there's a big balance between those four things."

That discussion seemed to help the Stansells. So did reading and discussing a magazine article their pastor gave them. Titled "The Victim of the Victimless Crime," it was the story of the wife of a pastor who had dealt with pornography and had confessed to his church board, gotten on with his life, and left his mate experiencing emotional devastation.

Kurt and Martha compared their own experience and tried to learn from the article. They both came to the understanding that he will never be "cured," that he'll face sexual temptations every day of his life. And while accountability will always be important, Martha needs to be part of that process. In coming to those conclusions, Martha affirmed Kurt by expressing appreciation for his honesty and the way he was working hard to conquer his addiction.

The Stansells didn't try to work through all their feelings at once. They couldn't have if they'd wanted to, because their reactions—especially Martha's—evolved through several stages. And each of those stages offered painful reminders to Kurt of what his behavior had cost.

For example, it took some weeks for Martha to process what Kurt had said that first night about how his actions had affected her self-image. "When I thought back," she says, "I realized I'd never remembered having self-image problems growing up. I'd always been a fairly confident person. But that had changed after we got married. Kurt always seemed so confident and articulate in comparison to me that whenever we had problems or tensions—sexually or in other areas—I'd just naturally assumed the problem was mine. There were times when he'd be critical of me for whatever reason, and I'd get even more nervous about that aspect of our relationship. After he told me about the topless dancers, I immediately remembered a time when I'd been getting undressed for bed and he'd asked me to do a little dance for him. I'd gotten embarrassed and told him I couldn't imagine doing that, and he had acted disappointed. I'd wondered what was wrong with me and what it was about me that so disappointed my husband. When I realized he had wanted me to reenact something he'd already seen some other woman do, it made me angry."

Martha says it also makes her angry to think about the sense of confusion she experienced over the years as a result of Kurt's mixed messages. "There'd be some nights when I'd feel romantic and want him, but Kurt would say he was too tired, and I just accepted that. I never really thought, *He doesn't love me anymore*. I took him at his word. I never suspected his erratic sexual interest in me was because he was getting some of his needs met in other ways. Sometimes I'd feel frustrated, but mostly I felt confused and gradually more and more insecure.

"Looking back, I feel mostly cheated. In some ways he may as well have had an affair, because it's much the same thing. He deceived me and often cheated me out of the chance to be the person to meet his sexual needs."

Kurt admits that as they had a variety of discussions about the issue over the following months, he, too, gained painful new insights into how his behavior had affected Martha and their relationship. "I realized God gave me a certain amount of sexual and relational energy," he says. "And He gave Martha her own commensurate needs. There should have been a direct correlation between the two. But because I was wasting a certain amount of my sexual interest and energy on the side for so many years, Martha had experienced a real deficiency in the attention and focused energy she'd received from me. I began to realize I needed to accept responsibility for that failure, and I determined to turn that around.

"For too long, instead of understanding my wife's sexual needs and working to meet them, I'd convinced myself that my own tolerance for sexual frustration was lower than hers, that my own needs were greater. If we hadn't made love for a week or so, I'd think, *Well for crying out loud, I obviously need sex more than she does*. That would become a rationalization for masturbation or for stimulation from pornography.

"Whenever Martha wanted to be intimate and I was already spent, it was a smack in the face because it made what I was giving up so obvious. The real thing with her was always better than any counterfeit or fantasy. The only true appeal of the fantasy was that it was always available—and without the work a real relationship took. It was simpler and easier. But it was always second best."

Martha says that's also part of what makes her feel cheated. At least to some extent because of his struggle with sexual addiction, Kurt and Martha had never communicated well about sexual matters. They're both working at doing better now. "I've recently told Kurt that I've often felt I've given more than I received in our sexual relationship," Martha says, "that I just wasn't experiencing a lot of pleasure. I never wanted to say that before for fear I'd hurt his feelings. So it sometimes makes me angry to realize a big part of the problem was that I wasn't the sole focus of his sexual attentions. Our sex life could have been so much better, but he had decided not to let it be.

"At least now I'm beginning to understand and experience some of what we were missing. I've become convinced in recent months that he is, indeed, committed to making every aspect of our relationship the best it can be. I'm gradually becoming confident enough to communicate my needs, and he's learning how to meet them."

Kurt and Martha are also starting to restore the trust that was lost when he first told her about the pornography. "As painful as his honesty was for both of us," she says, "I can see how that honesty is becoming the key for me to trust him more than I ever did before. I see the price he's willing to pay to be a man of integrity and to have the best possible relationship."

Kurt Stansell is quick to admit that the struggle isn't over—the war goes on. But he has found a number of weapons to use in his ongoing battle with temptation. The first is honesty and communication with his wife. They make those a high priority, even if some days they can take only five minutes in bed at night to ask, "Where are you tonight? Where are we?"

At the same time, Kurt believes strongly in the need for some other regular accountability—a guy like Stan whom he can go to without burdening Martha with the emotional load of his day-to-day temptations; someone he can call to say, "I'm feeling weak today" or "I feel a strong desire to go look at magazines today."

Kurt has also found that the darkness of sin is always alluring. "There's an ongoing temptation to ease up on the degree of honesty I have in my accountability relationship," he explains. "When things have been going well for a few weeks and then I slip up, it's easy to think, *I don't really need to bring that up.* That happened to me not long ago. And that evening after I'd met with Stan in the morning, I picked up my Bible and was reading in Psalm 32: 'Blessed is the man whose sin the LORD does not count against him. . . . Blessed is he whose transgressions are forgiven . . . and in whose spirit there is no deceit.' That hit me right between the eyes. But it went on to say, 'When I kept silent my bones wasted away. . . . I will confess my transgressions to the LORD—and you forgave the guilt of my sin.' And it was like *wow.* I had to call Stan right away and say, 'Here's where I am. I messed up. Here's what happened . . .'"

Another of Kurt's weapons is his devotional life. Honesty with God, just like honesty with his wife, is the key. He's working at being more transparent than ever before. He explains: "I'll say, 'Okay, Lord, I sense this seed of temptation in my heart today. I know I'm going on a business trip in two weeks, and as I think about that trip, I realize lots of things could happen. I want You to deal with that seed today.' The seed will probably be there every day for the rest of my life. But if God will help me constantly step on it and crush it, together we can keep that seed from germinating."

Still another weapon is Scripture memorization. Looking back, Kurt realizes he handled his addiction relatively well in college because at that time he was using memory-verse packs the Navigators publish on various topics, including overcoming temptation. So he has gone back to memorizing the Bible in recent months. He's working on the book of John and is already through chapter 7. "If I have trouble falling asleep," he says, "instead of fantasizing, I review verses. If I'm driving somewhere and see something that starts me thinking about things I shouldn't, I review verses. I heard a tape once where Chuck Swindoll talked about how the apostle Paul said that the weapons we fight with as Christians are not the weapons of the world—how Scripture can be used to destroy the strongholds of Satan and everything else that sets itself up against Christ. By using Scripture, 'we take captive every thought and make it obedient to Christ.' "

"My marriage now truly exceeds all the fantasies I ever had."

Last but certainly not least, Kurt is developing a level of trust in God that's deeper than ever. "I've finally learned that God's instructions for us are there for a reason," Kurt says. "He really does want what's best for me; He's not making up the rules arbitrarily. And when we follow His plan and work for His ideal, He amazes us with His blessing and the natural consequences that follow.

"For so many years, I thought I needed to look out for my own needs. But these past few months, I've learned that my relationship with my wife can meet all my sexual needs. My marriage now truly exceeds all the fantasies I ever had. It's so much more fulfilling to finally have a monogamous relationship with Martha than I ever dreamed it could be. It's challenging; it's fulfilling; it's exciting; it's rewarding. All those things I spent so many years looking for—excitement and escape—I now realize can only be found in committing myself to meeting Martha's needs. When I focus on her, I'm totally satisfied. It's an amazing thing. It makes me want to worship God and thank Him for His marvelous plan, and to thank Him that I finally learned the lesson. It was always there to be realized; I just finally submitted and decided to honor it."

Personal Evaluation

What one thing can you begin to do now to strengthen your defenses against sexual temptation (e.g., honesty with your wife, an accountability partner, memorize Scripture)?

In the Group

1. What did you try to do since the previous session to be a better father? How did it go?
2. What are some examples of our society's obsession with sex? Why this preoccupation?
3. How openly were sexual matters discussed in your childhood home? When and from whom did you learn about sex?
4. Kurt labels his problem an addiction. Would you agree or disagree? Why?
5. Kurt states that he believes he will probably always struggle with this problem. Do you agree, or do you think he should be able to get a once-and-for-all victory? Why? How does Kurt's view square with Romans 7:7-25 and 2 Corinthians 12:7-10?
6. Kurt also felt he needed to tell his wife about his problem. Is that always the right thing to do? Why or why not? What guidelines should be followed when a wife is informed? (See the advice Kurt's pastor gave him on p.141.)
7. Is this area a problem for you? If it is, how will you begin to address it? Who holds you accountable in this area?

My Response

If I'm totally honest with myself, I would have to say that my sexual life is

_____

_____

Memory Verse

"No temptation has seized you except what is common to man. And God is faithful; he will not let you be tempted beyond what you can bear. But when you are tempted, he will also provide a way out so that you can stand up under it" (1 Cor. 10:13).

CHAPTER 9

Introduction

As you read the following story, you'll be reminded that the greatest gift we can give to another is ourselves—our time and energy. You'll see, too, that when we do that, we find our own needs being met as well (see Gal. 6:7-10). And if we're hurting, this process can begin our healing.

What the man in this story did is nothing remarkable. But he was willing to be used by God in one boy's life, and God has used that willingness to forge a friendship that blesses them both. As you read the story, consider what small beginnings He might want you to make.

A Promise Keeper Allows God to Use Him

Ten-year-old Steven Isaacs is one of those kids the experts describe as "at risk." His single mom, an incest and rape victim in her youth, struggles to make ends meet. Though he regularly sees his father, a convicted felon no longer in prison, that relationship has its limitations. "Basically what I've learned from my dad," says Steven, "is how to blow bubbles with gum and eat Oreo cookies."

Thirty-one-year-old Gene Gregory has faced a few trials of his own. He struggled in his early adult years to integrate the principles learned during his Christian upbringing with the reality of the workaday world. Then, unable to find fulfilling work using his degree in psychology, Gene went back to school to pursue an entirely different career. That was the point at which his story began to intertwine with Steven's.

During the summer of 1993, Steven and his mother, Barbara, first heard about Promise Keepers while listening to a Focus on the Family broadcast. "I'd like to go to that conference in Boulder," Steven (only nine at the time) told his mom. She let the comment slide, figuring it was an impulsive, even predictable reaction of a young boy who would have jumped at any opportunity to visit the campus of his beloved Colorado University Buffaloes (only a few miles from his home in Denver).

The two of them had begun tuning in Christian radio programming only after Barbara had made a personal commitment to Christ a few months before. Steven had actually become a Christian before his mom. After reading the Bible stories he received as part of his home-school curriculum, he had given his heart to the Lord during a Christmas program at a local church.

Because of her son's new interest in spiritual things, Barbara had consented to attend church with him. It was there, when she got involved in a small Bible study group, that she soon became convicted of her own needs. So the two of them, both young Christians, found practical help and spiritual encouragement from Dr. James Dobson's radio show.

The conference in Boulder came and went, however, without Barbara ever following up on Steven's interest. They did listen to some of the live coverage on a local radio station. And when Dr. Dobson, speaking at the conference, said he thought every Christian man should have a conviction to be there, Steven turned to his mom and told her, "I have a conviction to go there, too."

Again his mom expected Steven's interest to wane, but when he kept talking about it in the months that followed, Barbara called the Promise Keepers national office to ask about the possibility of her son's going to the 1994 conference. What she learned was just what she expected: The conference was designed for men, though boys as young as 13 could attend if accompanied by their fathers.

Even that information failed to deter Steven. He decided to write a letter to Bill McCartney, coach of his favorite college football team and founder of Promise Keepers, explaining his desire to attend a conference. "I don't remember exactly what I said, and I didn't keep a copy of the letter," Steven says. "But it went something like this: 'Dear Coach McCartney, I am only nine years old, and I heard about Promise Keepers over the radio. I'd really like to go to the next conference, but supposedly you have to be 13. Can I come?' Then I added a P.S.: 'If I can't come, I hope you have a good reason.'

"I got a short note back saying, 'We'd love to have you come to the conference next year with your dad.' With the note, they sent me a Promise Keepers shirt and some more information about the organization. And on my birthday, a man from the Promise Keepers office came by to give me an autographed copy of Coach McCartney's book, *From Ashes to Glory*. That was really nice."

Steven was discouraged by the letter, however, because he doubted his father, Peter, would be willing to go with him. And even if he said he would go, Steven was reluctant to count on it. "He lives only a few blocks from us—

with my grandparents. So I see him fairly often. But a lot of times he'll say he's coming over or that we'll do something together, and then he'll change his mind. He'll call and say, 'Something came up' or 'I had something I had to do' or 'I'm gonna go out with some friends.' When that happens, when he's late or doesn't show up because his plans changed, he usually gives me some gift the next time I see him. Like he'll buy me X-Men things because he knows they're some of my favorite toys. He thinks stuff will make up for time. But it really doesn't."

Steven and Barbara continued to pray that somehow Steven would be able to go to Promise Keepers, that the Lord would work in Peter's heart and make him willing to go with his son. When the 1994 conference was still weeks away, they decided it was time to raise the subject.

"One day when we were together, I mentioned Coach McCartney and what he was doing with Promise Keepers," Steven recalls. "Dad said he'd heard something about that. I told him I wanted to go to the conference and asked if he'd be willing to go with me. 'I already have two tickets,' I told him. He said, 'Let me think about it.' But the way he said it didn't make me very hopeful. And the next time I saw him to ask again, he just said, 'Absolutely not!' He said he was going to have other things to do that weekend, but I could tell he just didn't want to go."

"My dad thinks stuff will make up for time. But it really doesn't."

Barbara Isaacs, unlike her son, never had much hope that Peter would agree to go. But because she saw how badly Steven wanted to attend Promise Keepers, she'd been considering other options.

She had become acquainted with Gene Gregory during the two years he and his wife, Tammy, had been bringing their two preschool daughters to the licensed day-care program Barbara operated out of her home. Of the families she served who would call themselves Christian, the Gregorys seemed to be living out their faith best. Barbara had been particularly impressed with Gene's commitment to spending time with his daughters even while he was working a full-time job and going to school to train for a new career. A couple times he had generously volunteered to help her do some handiwork around the house, too.

In addition to that, Gene had always seemed to take a special interest in

Steven. When he came to pick up his girls, if Steven had built something or had done something he was excited about, Gene would take a minute or two to hear him out. Sometimes he'd ask questions in response or let Steven show him what he'd been working on. Other parents were usually in a hurry when they came to pick up their kids. But because Gene treated Steven with respect and always had a little time for him, Steven liked him.

So Barbara began to consider asking Gene if he'd be willing to take Steven to Promise Keepers. "Because of things that happened to me as a girl, it's hard for me to want to trust someone with my child," Barbara admits. "But I'd known Gene and Tammy for almost two years. I'd been impressed by what I saw."

As sort of a trial run, Barbara asked Gene if he'd be willing to go with Steven to a father-son program her church was offering for preadolescent boys on "The Christian Male and Sexuality." She said she knew Steven's dad wouldn't be willing to go with him. She also knew she and her former husband no longer agreed on sexual values, so she wanted Steven to get some practical Christian teaching on the subject. And she wanted him to have a Christian man he could talk to about things he might not feel free to discuss with his mother.

When Barbara asked, Gene told her he thought it was great that the church had a program like that for boys Steven's age, and he immediately agreed to go with him. He and Steven had such a positive experience during the training sessions and playing basketball during breaks with the other men and boys that Barbara soon decided she would go ahead and ask Gene about escorting Steven to the Promise Keepers conference.

What little Gene had heard about the conference sounded interesting to him. So when Barbara explained Steven's interest and need for an adult escort, Gene didn't have to think long before telling her he'd go. He even insisted on paying his own way. "I figured if it meant that much to Steven, I'd be glad to make it possible," Gene says. "After all, in providing day-care for my daughters two days a week, his mother plays an important role in their lives. My wife and I considered the Isaacses almost part of our family."

Gene had heard enough of the Isaacses' story to know they'd been through rough times. He really admired Barbara for the way she was rearing Steven. Knowing how hard parenting was when he shared the load with his wife, Tammy, he could only imagine how tough a job Barbara had as a single mom.

And remembering the crucial role adult men played in his own life as a boy, Gene also felt for Steven.

"I learned the most important lessons in life from my father and my uncle," Gene says. "They taught me, both by word and by their examples, the Christian values I now try to live by. Plus they passed along all sorts of life skills—how to work hard, how to be responsible, and how to use my hands to fix and make things. I wouldn't be the person I am today if it hadn't been for their investment."

Accordingly, he saw Barbara's request as both an honor and an important responsibility. "But I had no idea how much that decision would mean to me and my family as well," he says.

Gene and Steven drove back and forth from Denver to Boulder for both days of the conference. "What an incredible experience Promise Keepers was!" Gene says. "To be there in a massive stadium packed with that many Christian men was in itself inspiring. Maybe because I was trying to see the event through Steven's eyes, I think I was as excited and awestruck as he was. He obviously was blown away by the crowd dynamics—the singing and the spirit of worship. So was I."

Gene was also struck by the sense of fellowship and harmony in the crowd. "I used to work concert security in college, so I've seen a lot of crowds," he says. "This one was unique." He was astonished when a man left his hat and wallet lying out on the ground for ten minutes, and they were still there, untouched, when he came back. "I know that by itself that seems like a small thing," Gene says. "But little things like that added up to make for one impressive testimony about integrity."

Steven got a big kick out of Chuck Swindoll riding out on a big Harley-Davidson and then seeing Gary Smalley arrive on stage straddling a little tricycle. But Gene wasn't sure how much of the actual teaching a 10-year-old boy could absorb. As they talked between sessions and on the drive back and forth from Denver, however, Gene realized just how perceptive Steven was and how much he remembered of what the speakers said.

Yet Gene thinks he got even more out of it than Steven. Many of the speakers put into words a lot of feelings about the Christian faith that he'd had all his life, driving home lessons his dad and uncle had taught. "I particularly remember the challenge put to us as fathers: That our kids are the only things of importance we're going to leave behind on this earth when we die," he says.

"None of the things we accumulate or recognition we receive is going to matter. So we need to fulfill our responsibility to give our children the time and energy and affirmation that will assure them they're special. And we need to teach them about God and what it really means to have a relationship with Christ, as well as to show them how to find guidance and comfort in His Word."

Gene says attending Promise Keepers with Steven moved their relationship to a new level as well. They felt a sense of oneness there. "Steven knew, without my having to say it, that I wasn't there just because I was taking him," Gene says. "He could see that the experience meant something significant in my life, and I saw that it was making a real impact on him. We shared a powerful spiritual experience, which is something we'll remember all our lives. To have that in common is a neat bond between us now."

It was late before Steven and Gene got back each evening. "But the two of them were higher than a kite both nights," Barbara remembers. "They were so up from the conference, it was fun to listen to everything they wanted to tell me. Gene said that having Steven there really added to the conference for him—especially the session where Howard Hendricks talked about the impact mentors can have."

"I'd like to do that—to be a mentor for Steven," Gene said. And in the weeks to come, that began to happen. Gene says he hasn't found as much time as he'd like to spend with Steven—at least not big blocks of time. "Time always seems tough to come by," he admits. But he's found it in bits and pieces, making a point to take a minute or two with the boy whenever he sees him and looking for occasional chances to include him in a Gregory family activity—whether that's a special outing or just an evening at home playing games. A couple times, Gene and his wife have taken Steven on a Saturday just to give Barbara time for herself. And Gene thrilled Steven by taking him to a Colorado Buffalo football game.

"I've discovered it really doesn't matter what you're doing," Gene says. "For example, we built a bookcase together for his room. I got to teach Steven a few fundamentals about woodworking. Whatever we do together can be a tool to make points with."

Gene also talks with Steven about the superhero play Steven's into. "I had my own superheroes as a kid," Gene says, "so I can relate. But he knows very well that superheroes are just fantasy—that there's only one true Superhero, and that's Jesus."

Being with Steven has made Gene aware of how much a boy needs at least one good example. "And it needs to be a man," Gene says. "Steven's mom does a great job. But Steven's stuck being a male, and he's going to learn how to be a man, not from his mother, but mostly from the other men in his life." This mentor doesn't have to be perfect, Gene stresses—"I'm certainly not." But he does need to be someone who is honest about life's hard times and who, in the midst of them, doesn't give up his beliefs but is true to his relationships with his family and his God.

> ### *"Steven's going to learn how to be a man, not from his mother, but mostly from the other men in his life."*

"A boy needs to see," Gene continues, "that no matter what happens, this man is going to lean on God, and that is what will get him through. He needs to see a man who isn't copping out and running from responsibility. He needs to see a man who's a cheerful worker and who does all these things because it's the best way, because it works, because these are the things that hold civilization together."

Gene is grateful that his own father and uncle gave him that kind of example. As a youth, his dad had several different men who filled that role in his life, teaching him that "this truth, this faith, this God you can believe in—these are constant things you can count on in your worst days."

Not long ago, when Gene was talking with his father, his dad said, "You know, Gene, when you talk about this boy Steven, it reminds me of myself at that age. I think of those men who took me under their wings and how much it meant in my life. So I want to tell you, son, you're doing a wonderful thing here."

"For my dad to say that to me, showing me how God has brought things full circle, moved me to tears," Gene says.

But his dad's approval hasn't been the only affirmation Gene has received. Not long into his relationship with Steven, Barbara told Gene that her son had confided in her that if he could have any man in the world to be his dad, Gene was near the top of the list—right along with James Dobson and Bill McCartney. When he heard that, says Gene, "Not only was I flattered, but at that moment, I realized what an awesome and beautiful responsibility I

had. I realized I needed to be in this for the long haul. I could never inten-
tionally let Steven down because of the way he's looking at me."

At the same time, Gene is careful not to try to replace or criticize Steven's
dad. He hopes, in fact, that his working with Steven will somehow help bring
Steven and Peter closer together. And Barbara says that's happening.
Recently her ex-husband told her that he wants Steven to like and respect
him "the way he does Gene." So Barbara told him, "Gene's earned that by
being honest with Steven, by being dependable, by communicating with him,
and by being there for Steven."

That conversation seemed to make an impression. Barbara says that in the
past, Peter's idea of time together with his son was to watch a movie
together—something that required no real interaction. But that's changing; he seems to be listening and paying more personal attention to Steven
now. "So far I think the obvious influence Gene has with Steven has made
his father want to try harder," Barbara adds. "He's been trying to clean up his
act a little. We all keep hoping and praying that maybe he'll even agree to
go with Gene and Steven to next year's Promise Keepers conference.
Wouldn't that be something?"

Both Barbara and Gene are also heartened by the impact all this continues to have on Steven. Barbara was so impressed that she wrote Promise
Keepers a letter, filling them in on the story and letting them know how
much the organization had influenced her boy. To show how much Steven
had gotten out of the conference itself, she included in her letter a copy of
the notes he took while listening to the various speakers. He'd written:

> Don't mock God.
>
> Don't abandon God.
>
> You reap what you sow.
>
> Don't give God deviled eggs.
>
> Make a 180 turn.
>
> Stand up for Jesus.
>
> In the eyes of the Lord, we are one.
>
> Jesus is coming.
>
> This is the moment.

The land is there, but it is occupied.

We are men of God.

Now is the time.

Have a mentoring relationship.

Everybody has a place.

Spend prime time with God.

In God's Word we grow.

Families are a top priority.

Have a holy heart.

Run away from sin.

Accept responsibility.

Be accountable.

Are you spending time with God?

"As you can see," Barbara wrote, "Steven listened closely and learned a lot."

Gene, too, has been impressed by his young friend's sensitivity and insight. When they were at the CU football game, Steven commented, "You know, some people spend so much time on football that they neglect their families." Once when they saw an ad for a new car, he observed, "You need to have a car you can count on to get you where you need to go, but to spend that much money on a car . . . Well, there are a lot more important things you can do with money—like help other people."

Gene just shakes his head and says, "He comes up with stuff like that all the time. He's always thinking. He's concerned about his dad's spiritual condition. And now that his grandfather has cancer, Steven worries about the quality of time his dad is spending with his grandfather. It makes me proud just to watch him growing up."

Barbara has been so touched by Gene's obvious commitment to her son that she asked if he'd be willing to become Steven's legal guardian if anything should happen to her. She worried that Peter still wouldn't be responsible enough to handle single parenthood. And she knew that neither he nor any of her other relatives shared her Christian values or would have any real commitment to helping Steven continue to grow spiritually.

Gene said he'd talk to Tammy, but he knew even before he did what her answer would be. Tammy, too, had grown up with a sense of strong family values; she respected what Gene was trying to do for Steven. Because she saw the sense of fulfillment her husband received from his relationship with Steven, she had never resented the time Gene invested in the boy. In truth, their relationship was an enriching asset to the whole Gregory family. Not only had Gene's commitment to Steven made him a more thoughtful father to their daughters, but Steven had become a loving "big brother" to the girls. His mom had become an honorary member of their extended family as well, with the Isaacses sharing an evening meal with the Gregorys at least once a month.

"After Tammy and I talked, I got back to Barbara and told her I expected her to outlive me," Gene says. "But I also told her I was honored by her request and would be glad to serve as Steven's guardian if that need ever arose. While I realized that could be quite a responsibility, I'd be glad to do it. I've benefited so much from my relationship with Steven already. He worries about me. He cares about me. He listens. Plus I get to see myself in him a little, and that's fun. I get the satisfaction of being able to say the things to him that I wish someone had said to me when I was his age. I get to pass along all the lessons my dad taught me that have made a difference in my life. I don't have to be Steven's dad, just his friend. And that's wonderful enough."

Gene concludes, "If I could say one thing to other men about mentoring, it's that the rewards far outweigh the costs. To know that you're making a difference in a young life is reward beyond measure. But to know and feel the respect and admiration of a kid like Steven—wow! I don't deserve it, but what a gift!"

Personal Evaluation

Read each of the following statements, and then, on a scale from 1 (totally disagree) to 10 (totally agree), rate how you respond:

___ 1. I tend to live my life with the needs of others in mind.

___ 2. I could never mentor someone else's child.

___ 3. The idea of giving my life for another makes me uncomfortable.

___ 4. Steven's dad should take responsibility so Gene can concentrate on his own problems.

___ 5. I believe I can make a difference with my one life.

___ 6. I have enough concerns of my own to worry about.

___ 7. I have difficulty deciding where and how I can make a difference.

In the Group

1. What was your greatest temptation in the area of sexual purity in the last week? How did you handle it?

2. Which traits of Steven's are worth emulating? Why?

3. What fears or hesitations do you think Gene had to overcome to pursue his friendship with Steven? What fears might Gene's wife have had? His children? Steven's mom?

4. How can we develop more of a mind-set of seeking to meet the needs of others?

5. Ephesians 3:20 says God is able to do more through us than we can even imagine. Do you really believe God could use you like a Gene, beyond what you can now foresee? Why or why not?

6. Is your own child a person to whom you need to do more reaching out? Why or why not? How about a grandchild?

7. Name one young person outside your immediate family—the child of a single-parent friend, neighbor, relative, or person in your church—whom you could befriend.

8. Close by praying that God will help each group member see how He wants to use you in someone else's life.

My Response

One thing I got out of this story and discussion is _____
_____

An initial step I could take this week to reach out to the young person
in #6 or #7 above is _____
_____

Memory Verse

"Now to him who is able to do immeasurably more than all we ask or
imagine, according to his power that is at work within us . . . " (Eph. 3:20).

CHAPTER 10

Introduction

In some small New England towns, the most popular tourist attraction is the local cemetery. As you walk along and read the centuries-old gravestones, you'll see humorous sayings (apparently written by less-than-generous spouses), sad words telling of the death of a child or other loved one, and serious messages with profound meaning.

Have you ever wondered what will be placed on your burial marker? When you die, how will you have spent the one life God has entrusted to you? What motivates you day by day? Is it a desire to be liked or to be happy? Will people say that you grabbed hold of everything you could?

For us Christians, God has a different plan. He says that it's in giving that we receive, in losing that we gain. What a novel idea! Instead of living me-centered lives, we're called by God to other-centered living. And when we accept that call, it's amazing what He can and will do through one person, or one church, to reach out to a hurting world.

A Promise Keeper Touches His World

I t all started simply enough one Sunday after the morning worship service. A first-time visitor to Pastor Van Roland's Portland, Oregon, church introduced himself and his family. Joe told Van that he'd been brought to Portland by a local Christian organization interested in developing a group home for people with AIDS.

"The moment I heard that, something struck a chord in my heart," Van says. "I told him, 'That sounds like something I'd be interested in learning more about.'"

A short while later, the two men met for lunch, and Joe went into more detail about his vision for a residential facility, a seven- or eight-bed group home where AIDS patients could live (and die) with dignity, cared for in a warm, loving environment. Van said he would help in any way he could.

He had no idea how that friendly offer would change his ministry, his church, and his life.

A couple weeks later, Joe called and asked, "Are you ready to get your feet wet on this issue?" He told Van he had made an appointment to visit a local AIDS facility, a secular group home for people with AIDS, and he wondered if Van would like to go along. Van said he would.

In the meantime, the Portland newspaper ran a story about the plans Joe's organization had to build an AIDS home as part of a Christian ministry. In response to that article, Joe received a call from a woman who wanted to know, "When is your house going to open?"

When Joe told her the opening was still months away, she said, "That's too bad, because my sister Cindy, a Christian woman who has been a missionary to Australia, is dying of AIDS. I was hoping we could get her into a Christian environment, because the home where she is now isn't Christian at all."

When he learned where this woman's sister was, Joe said, "Believe it or not, I've got an appointment to visit that very home tomorrow. And I'm taking a local pastor with me."

The woman asked the pastor's name, and when she heard "Van Roland," she couldn't believe it. She had attended a former church of Van's in another city more than 10 years earlier.

"We'll be sure to visit your sister tomorrow," Joe promised. The woman excitedly thanked him, seeing this as an answer to her prayers for her sister.

When Joe and Van arrived at the AIDS facility the next day, the woman had already called and gotten their names on her sister's visitor list. So they went to her room.

Cindy was clearly in the advanced stages of AIDS. Once a tall, strong woman, she was now reduced to skin and bones. She'd lost most of her hair and exhibited open sores. She was already experiencing dementia as well. While she managed to tell her visitors about her three children, she couldn't remember their ages (16, 14, and nine). "My husband died two years ago as a result of AIDS contracted from IV drug use before he became a Christian," she said.

"Cindy wasn't very pleasant to look at," Van says. "But the Lord gave me a love for her from the beginning. And maybe because I was a pastor, she warmed to me right away. I laid my hands on her and prayed for her. And then I just held her and promised that I'd be a pastor to her from then on, that I'd visit her and try to support her."

Van visited Cindy regularly for the remaining four months of her life. He'd sit and talk with her. Sometimes she would be tired, so he would help her lie down, cover her with a blanket, and read the Bible to her until she fell asleep. He'd pray for her and her children. "Sometimes she wouldn't even awaken to know I was there," Van says. "But I'd sit by her bed for a while, watching and praying for her."

One of the first times Van visited, he noticed Cindy had a CD player. After looking through her small CD collection, he asked if she'd like some good praise music. "That would be wonderful," she said. So Van went to a local Christian bookstore and explained the situation, and the manager donated a CD that became a source of comfort to Cindy and her family in the last months of her life.

"That's how it began for me," Van says, explaining that the time he spent with Cindy over those few months was every bit as much a blessing to him as it was to her. "It started me on a road I never expected to travel as I became convinced the Lord wanted me to become involved in AIDS ministry and to influence others to become involved as well."

Van began to speak publicly in his church about the need and opportunities for an AIDS ministry. He encouraged people to be especially supportive of Joe's Christian group-home project because there wasn't anything else like it in that part of the country.

One couple in Van's church came to the first informational meeting. Because they saw their pastor and their church taking a compassionate stand, they brought along a brother, Frank, who was confined to a wheelchair by the final stages of AIDS. Van asked him if he had a pastor. When Frank said he didn't, Van told him he'd be glad to be his pastor.

So Van began visiting Frank in the same group home where Cindy had been. Frank grew steadily weaker and sicker. "Sometimes I'd want to read him a passage of Scripture, but he would tell me he just wasn't up to it," Van says. "So I would say, 'Okay, Frank.' After all, I was there to meet his needs, not to make myself feel good."

One day when Van knew Frank didn't have long to live, Van rolled Frank's wheelchair out on the deck where they could be alone. "There in the warm sunshine, I confessed to him some of the things I'd been involved in before I came to Christ," Van says.

"You know what?" Frank said. "That makes me like you even better."

"How so?" Van asked.

"Because I think you can understand me having been gay." And then he asked the question Van had wanted him to ask for so long: "What made you change?"

"I told him my testimony of how I came to Christ," Van says. "When I finished, I asked, 'Frank, how would you like to really know in your heart that Christ loves you, that you are His, and that there's no doubt where you're going when you die?'"

Frank nodded his head seriously, and Van took his frail hand. With his other hand, Van began to rub Frank's head. "I wanted him to know I wasn't afraid to touch him despite the sores all over his face and body," Van says. "We prayed together, and when we finished, he had big tears in his eyes. I told him, 'Frank, you are now my brother in Christ. When you leave here, you're going to be going ahead of me into the presence of Jesus Christ.'"

"I believe that," Frank said. Three days later, he died.

During those first months of ministry to people like Cindy and Frank, Van attended the weekend Promise Keepers conference in Boulder, Colorado. That experience intensified his growing conviction about involving himself and his church in AIDS ministry. He saw direct application in the underlying Promise Keepers theme of unity. He explains, "If we as a church (universal and in our local congregations) truly want to be the living body that Jesus wants us to be, then the denominational walls, the racial walls, and all the other walls we've erected to separate us from each other have to come down.

> *"If we truly want to be the living body that Jesus wants us to be, then all the walls we've erected to separate us from each other have to come down."*

"I believe that's what happened in the early church, where no one was excluded. The world took notice and said, 'What is it about these Christians?' And as a result, the Lord added to the church daily 'those who were being saved.' We need to open our church doors today and invite people in, saying, 'We don't care who you are, what you've done, what religious background you come from, what color you are, or whether you're gay or straight. If you want to know God, if you want to grow spiritually, this is the place for you. You'll be loved and cared for here.' People will notice and be drawn to that kind of attitude."

That's exactly what began happening in the case of Van Roland and Seven Hills Church. As the time approached for the official opening of the new Christian group home for AIDS patients, Joe asked Van to become a volunteer caregiver at the home and to help train others. Several people from his congregation volunteered as the whole church caught this vision for reaching out to the local community in a way no other church was doing. "As the Lord burdened my heart," Van says, "He also began connecting me with other people who wanted to minister or needed to be ministered to, both inside and outside our congregation."

Van met a woman whose son had died of AIDS five years earlier. She and her husband had formed an organization to help people with HIV/AIDS-infected loved ones. Would his church be willing to provide a meeting place for a Christian support group for families dealing with AIDS? And would he be willing to help her lead the group? Van told her yes on both counts.

One night some weeks later, Van received a phone call from Charlie, a prominent member of his church—a dynamic, young professional man who was active in a Christian music ministry. He asked Van, "Could you and your wife come over and meet with us tonight? I've been sick the last couple days and had a dramatic weight loss. I've just come back from the doctor's office, and I'd like to talk to you."

Even as he hung up the phone, Van knew what his friend was going to tell him. He said to his wife, Helen, "I believe Charlie has AIDS." Helen only looked at him in disbelief.

When Van and Helen walked in the front door of Charlie and Kim's house a short while later, Van's suspicions were instantly confirmed. "When I saw the sober look on their faces and the look of pain and almost terror in Kim's eyes, I knew without a doubt what they were going to say. They'd come from the doctor's office not two hours earlier. The doctor had told them it would take 10 to 12 days to get the official test results, but that he'd interned in San Francisco and had no doubts about the diagnosis."

Charlie told Van that after hearing him teach about ministering to people with AIDS and seeing the church's response, Van had been the first person he called. "By this time we were all weeping and hugging each other," Van says. "And Charlie went on to say that he wanted to go public with this before our whole congregation 'because I know how I'm going to be treated; I know how I'm going to be accepted.'"

Van assured Charlie and Kim that he would do whatever he could to support them in that decision. But first they would need to tell their families, and before that they would need confirmation of Charlie's blood tests.

Van also told Kim she should be tested as well. She hadn't thought of that. And Van promised that if they wanted, he and Helen would be glad to go with them to the doctor when they got their test results back. For the next couple of weeks, Van was in contact with Charlie and Kim every day. They would talk on the phone, or he would stop by their house and have coffee or just talk for a while.

When Charlie asked his doctor if it would be all right for his pastor to come with him to get the test results, the doctor said that would be fine. But he also expressed his surprise, saying, "I've never seen this happen before. That a pastor would come in with someone like this!"

"Well, that's the kind of church I go to!" Charlie told him.

The doctor couldn't hide his amazement when the day finally came and Van showed up with Charlie and Kim. Van told the doctor about his and the congregation's involvement with AIDS ministry. "I could see as we chatted that our conversation was breaking down some walls and shattering some stereotypes that doctor seemed to have about evangelical Christians," Van says. "And I remember him smiling and saying, 'This is really good to hear. I'm so pleased to know the kind of emotional and spiritual support Charlie is going to get from his church.'"

Then the doctor told Charlie his AIDS test had come back positive. Van looked immediately at Charlie and squeezed his hand. Then he squeezed Kim's. "Charlie took it well," Van says. "He was very courageous. He just said, 'Well, I was prepared for this.'"

The doctor set the next appointment and told Charlie he recommended starting treatments with the anti-HIV drug AZT. Then Charlie, Kim, and Van left the doctor's office together.

They got to the parking lot before Kim broke down. "I felt like a father almost," Van says. "I took them both in my arms and hugged them, and Kim cried and cried. Then Charlie began to express his concern for Kim, which was amazing. He reassured her, 'We're going to get through this. It'll be okay.'"

Van said, "Charlie, you've got to be honest with me now. If this is tough for you, don't pretend that you're okay."

"No, really, I'm not pretending," Charlie said. "I feel God's strength. I feel supported, and with you just being here today, the load is lighter."

Van was reminded at that moment of the apostle Paul's words encouraging believers to "bear one another's burdens and so fulfill the law of Christ." Van says, "It's mysterious, but it really does happen. When we pray with somebody, when we go and support somebody in a situation like that, the unbearable load gets distributed on other shoulders. That's what was happening for Charlie. He didn't have to feel the weight of this thing all alone. It was truly my privilege as his pastor to help bear his load."

Fortunately, Kim's test results came back negative. And a few days after that, Van and Helen sat in Charlie and Kim's living room as the young couple broke the news to their parents and siblings. "They received overwhelming support from their families," Van recalls. "As we all embraced and cried together, I assured their parents that we wanted to help take really good care of their kids, and that Charlie and Kim would not lack for support or love from their church friends."

Before breaking the news to the congregation, however, Van consulted a lawyer. Because of laws protecting the privacy of anyone with HIV or AIDS, he knew he needed to obtain legal disclosure permission before publicly revealing anyone's HIV status; otherwise, the church could be subject to federal fines. That done, arrangements were made to tell the congregation.

On the appointed Sunday, Charlie's parents and brothers came again from Minnesota and sat in the front row. At the end of the service, a carefully worded statement was read to the congregation. It said, in effect, that because of lifestyle choices made several years in the past, Charlie had been diagnosed as HIV positive. Charlie had already sought the Lord's forgiveness for those behaviors that he had long ago abandoned. Further, the pastoral staff was standing 100 percent behind Charlie and Kim. And because of the kind of church they belonged to, Charlie and Kim wanted their church family to know about the situation. Charlie didn't want to hide—nor did he feel he needed to hide—this fact, and he wanted to continue his normal ministry activities in the church.

"When we finished reading the statement," Van continues, "without any cue, the entire congregation—about 1,200 or 1,300 people there that day—stood to their feet and for I don't know how long gave Charlie and Kim a standing ovation. You could just sense God's blessing, as if God were saying, 'I am pleased in this.' The feeling was incredible."

Then they had Charlie and Kim come and stand at the front with the pastoral staff. "Those of you who are close friends with Charlie and Kim," Van said, "we want you to come forward, and we're going to pray for them and for their family." There wasn't enough room for the people who came forward. After the prayer, Van said, "If you want to come and personally give your affirmation to Charlie and Kim, we want to give you opportunity to do that." So they formed a receiving line, and people kept coming for an hour. "We closed the service," Van says, "but people sat down. They didn't want to leave. You could just feel this presence of the Lord's glory and love. People were hugging each other. Others were talking. There were some people still in the building at 2:00 that afternoon."

At one point Van looked out in the congregation and saw a young man whose wife came to the support group. Van had been trying to make connection with him for some time. The man had developed AIDS but hadn't been willing to tell anyone, and he hadn't been in church for a year. He "just happened" to be in the service that day. Van noticed he was watching the whole scene with astonishment.

The next day he called Van to ask, "Would you and your wife come to our house for dinner? I want to talk with you."

Van and Helen went, and from that dinner has now developed a close friendship. Van is caring for the man one on one, "and since then he's been coming to the church," Van says. "Very recently, he came to his first support-group meeting with his wife."

"Any number of people have come in and revealed things in their lives because they feel they can be vulnerable in our church now."

In the first evening service after Charlie's disclosure, a lay leader took Van aside and, with tears in his eyes, said, "You know, when you first got involved in AIDS ministry, I thought, *That's good for Pastor Van. That's probably something he feels he needs to do.* But I look back on these past few months—the things you've taught, the church's support and involvement with the group home, the support group—and now, all of a sudden, here are Charlie and Kim with this need. God has been preparing our church, hasn't He?"

"You're right," Van told him. "This thing is a lot bigger than you and me."

If anything, the congregation has grown *more* serious about AIDS ministry as a result of Charlie and Kim's announcement. More than 30 people have been trained as volunteer caregivers at the Christian group home. The average attendance at the support group has risen to about 20. The church is shattering stereotypes (sometimes justly earned, Van says) "that we Christians sit in our comfortable pews behind walls that protect us like a fort, taking potshots at all the people and things in the world we don't like."

Van declares, "It has been incredible. When we really reach out to the world in love, when we stretch to that farthest point, it's like stretching out a big tent. When we say, 'We're going to stand with people who have AIDS and love and care for them,' we stretch that tent to cover a lot of other people in the process.

"Since that Sunday when we presented Charlie and Kim's situation to the congregation, I've gotten phone calls. I've gotten faxes. I've gotten appointments. Any number of people have come in and revealed things in their lives because they feel they can be vulnerable in our church now."

One woman came and told Van she had had three abortions and was involved in cocaine, but now she wanted to make her life right with Jesus Christ. A man—a prominent member of the church—told Van he was working out the issues of homosexuality and was now seeking counseling. Van gave him a hug and said, "You know what? I love you even more."

"You do?" the man said.

"Yes, because you've trusted me with a great trust," Van said.

"There are just so many needs," Van says earnestly. "And we make a serious mistake when we think of them as 'out there' because they are so often right here in our churches. AIDS is only one of the needs, but the Centers for Disease Control estimate that one in every 250 Americans is HIV positive and doesn't yet know it because it has a seven- to 10-year incubation period. There are even bigger percentages of people in our pews every Sunday suffering over other issues—afraid to reveal their pain for fear of ostracism or harsh judgment. If we stretch out our tents far enough to cover them all with the love of God, breaking past all the barriers, it will revolutionize our churches."

According to Van, there are also personal ramifications to such ministry. As a result of his experience in recent months, he says, "I'm not the same man I was a year ago. I always felt I was a compassionate, loving pastor. But God has shown me that I need to love even more and reach out even further if I'm going to be the man He wants me to be. If I'm willing to do that, He'll turn my life inside out and help me grow.

"God has been teaching me that reaching out should become an almost involuntary reflex. You know how, when you accidentally hit your thumb with a hammer, it suddenly hurts so much that your entire body focuses on the pain in your thumb? I'm convinced that only when we begin to respond that instinctively to the pain in the world around us will we start being a truly healthy body of Christ."

Personal Evaluation

The thought of holding someone other than a family member who is dying of AIDS makes me feel _____

_____

In the Group

1. Did you take the first step in reaching out that you wrote in your response section for the last session? If so, what happened? If not, when can you plan to do it?
2. What individuals or groups of people would you find it difficult to minister to? Why?
3. How do you think your church would respond to the idea of an AIDS ministry? a ministry to the homeless? Why?
4. In what ways are you already seeking to make a difference in your world?
5. What are some specific, currently unmet needs in your community that you could help with? that your church could help meet?
6. If a fellow Christian were hesitant to get involved with some kind of outreach to the community, what Scripture passages would you use to show him that such outreach is pleasing to God?

My Response

One lesson I learned from this story is _____

_____

One area of outreach I believe God might want me to explore is

_____

_____

Memory Verse

"The King will reply, 'I tell you the truth, whatever you did for one of the least of these brothers of mine, you did for me' " (Matt. 25:40).

CHAPTER 11

Introduction

The story of Bud Schaedel, first told briefly at the Anaheim, California, Promise Keepers conference in 1994, summarizes many of the elements of what it means to raise the standard and be a man of integrity in every situation and every relationship. Bud didn't do any one spectacular thing. Instead, day in and day out, he simply chose to honor God by loving his wife, serving his pastor, studying the Bible, and encouraging and challenging brother Christians to be Promise Keepers, too. Yet the impact of his life will only be fully known in heaven.

As you read this story of an ordinary man with an extraordinary God, told here in depth for the first time, be thinking about how that same Almighty God might want to use you.

A Promise Keeper Honors God
Above All Else

You may have lymphoma, Bud," the grim-faced doctor said. "I'd like to refer you to a cancer specialist at Cedars-Sinai Medical Center in Los Angeles." Bud Schaedel was one of those people who had been blessed with life-long good health. On rare occasions he caught some kind of bug, but he never let it slow him down or even force him to miss a day of work. That was just the kind of guy he was—a full-speed-ahead sort of personality.

When Bud got out of the Navy at the age of 21, one of his officers wrote him a letter of recommendation guaranteeing that he'd be "an asset to any organization" and citing Bud's "integrity, honesty, and hard work." Those characteristics served him well in the industrial paint manufacturing business where he immediately proved himself management material and rapidly worked his way up the corporate ladder. He became a sales manager in the Midwest, then a plant manager in the Pacific Northwest, before taking over the operation of yet another large facility in Southern California in the mid-1980s.

Right after Christmas 1989, however, Bud came down with the flu, and a week or so later he noticed swelling in the glands along his neck. His doctor prescribed a couple rounds of antibiotics, but the swelling remained, so he ordered blood tests. Then came the terrible diagnosis.

Bud appeared outwardly unfazed by the news, but his wife, Connie, barely held her composure in the doctor's office. And when the two of them walked out and climbed into their car, she lost it completely. "I dissolved into a blubbering idiot," she says. This was Bud, the man who had healed her deep emotional wounds and who had never stopped courting her!

"Let's don't jump to conclusions," he told her gently, trying to comfort them both. "Nothing is certain yet. Let's hear what the experts say." Still, every day seemed an eternity until the appointment with the specialist.

Before Connie and Bud met, they had both known the pain and frustration of a failed marriage relationship. Bud's daughter was grown and married and his son was almost ready to graduate from high school when he was divorced from his first wife.

The vicious and spiteful conflict that marked Connie's divorce left her with gaping emotional wounds and scars of bitterness. When her former husband made good on his threats to fight for and win custody of their two young children, she experienced a depth of raw pain she had never before imagined. Swearing off men, marriage, and the whole concept of romantic love, Connie channeled her energies into her job as a production assistant in the facility Bud ran.

At first, Connie rebuffed even the most casual expressions of friendliness on Bud's part. Then gradually, amazingly, and against all odds, Bud's unrelenting friendliness, interest, and acceptance began to crack her protective shell. Ever so slowly, Connie opened her heart enough to believe she could love again. She even started to smile and laugh once more. When Bud asked her to marry him, she said yes.

Perhaps because he was determined to have a better marriage and be a better husband than he had been the first time around, perhaps because he sensed Connie's desperate need for a steady dose of love to heal her old hurts and erase her lingering doubts, Bud never quit treating her like a queen. Virtually every morning they were together, he would slip out of bed while she was still sleeping, fix her a cup of coffee, and bring it to her in bed with the "Love Is" cartoon from the newspaper. Sometimes he would even pencil in a few words of his own. And if they were out of town and he couldn't get a paper, he would draw his own cartoon. Over the years, his constant supply of unconditional love mended wounds Connie thought would never be closed. "His love was an unspeakable gift to me," she says.

Yet Bud and Connie's idyllic world seemed ready to collapse around them that day in the doctor's office. The subsequent trip to see the specialist brought good news and bad. The bad news came when the original diagnosis was confirmed. The good news was that Bud's case was "chronic lymphoma." The doctor assured Bud and Connie that he had patients who had lived with Bud's form of the disease for years with little change in their quality of life. His recommended treatment was regular monitoring and periodic chemotherapy if and when any serious flare-up occurred.

Connie was somewhat relieved, but she couldn't help thinking, *What would I do if I ever lost this man I've grown to love so much!*

Meanwhile, Bud charged ahead. His health remained unchanged for almost a year. And while Connie's concern for him never left her mind completely, Bud allowed his illness to have little impact on his daily routines. He told few people about the lymphoma, choosing to go on as if nothing were wrong. The only change Connie saw was Bud's increased interest in the spiritual realm of life. He was praying and reading the Bible more than he had in many years.

During his first marriage, Bud had been active in a church in Indianapolis, a tireless worker on any and every committee. He had even preached an occasional sermon when the pastor was gone.

But after Connie and Bud married and moved to the Pacific Northwest, he began a long period of spiritual drifting. The Schaedels occasionally attended a church near their home, but they never seemed to connect there, and neither Connie nor Bud got very involved. When they moved to Southern California in the mid-'80s, they hadn't found even a nominal church home. But now, suddenly faced with cancer's undeniable reminder of his mortality, Bud evidenced a growing spiritual hunger.

Bud assured her, "I have a strong feeling that God isn't through with me yet."

In the winter of 1991, when the lymphoma flared up and the doctors began the first round of chemotherapy, Bud seemed to have a new and growing sense of peace. The chemo had no impact, however, and Connie grew more and more panicky. "Oh, Bud, I'm so scared!" she told him tearfully. "What are we going to do?"

Bud assured her, "I have a strong feeling that God isn't through with me yet," and somehow his unwavering confidence calmed her fears.

As they finally began talking about his condition with friends and relatives, many called or wrote to say they were praying for Bud and had added his name to their prayer chains. Bud told Connie that some days he thought he could feel the effects of their prayers. And those prayers, plus a second round of chemo with a new experimental drug, finally did the trick. Bud's lymphoma went into remission.

Shortly after that, Bud and Connie spent some vacation time with a couple of longtime friends from their Indiana days. This man, like Bud, had drifted away from church attendance, so Bud asked him why. Each time he gave a reason, Bud played devil's advocate and pressed him to explain. The fellow got more and more frustrated until finally he said, "Look, are you trying to embarrass me or make me feel guilty or what!"

"I apologize," Bud said, sorry he'd pushed so hard. "Uh, I think I need a drink of water." And with that he escaped into the kitchen. When Connie followed him there, he told her, "I guess I've just heard every excuse I've ever made for not going to church, and I've got to change that."

In looking for a church, the Schaedels remembered how much they had enjoyed Willow Creek Community Church when they had visited Connie's brother in Chicago's northwest suburbs. So they wrote him to ask if he could recommend a Southern California church that might be similar in style. After some digging, he told them about a church near them called Whittier Area Baptist Fellowship (WABF).

The next morning, just hours after hearing from Connie's brother, a flier fell out of the newspaper Bud was reading. When he picked it up, he couldn't believe his eyes. "Look at this!" he exclaimed. It was a listing of programs offered by WABF. The Schaedels quickly agreed, "This *can't* be a coincidence. We'd better check this one out."

The following Sunday, they sat on the second row, and they both immediately felt at home. Bud had a sense of kinship with and respect for Pastor Lee Eliason. And those feelings only deepened in the weeks that followed as the Schaedels became regular attendees. Bud, who had always prided himself on being an analytical and rational person, frequently found himself moved by the music and the message he was hearing. What he'd believed in his head for years was somehow touching his heart.

The more spiritual food he devoured, the hungrier Bud seemed for more. For the first time in his life, he began listening to a Christian radio station as he drove to and from work. It was there that he first heard about something called a Promise Keepers conference. He caught parts of the ad two or three times and heard just enough to be intrigued. But he didn't get a clear idea of what Promise Keepers was or what was going to happen at the conference planned for that summer in Colorado.

Late that spring of 1993, Bud casually asked one of the church staff members what he knew about Promise Keepers and its upcoming conference. The man's face lit up, his eyes zeroed in on Bud's, and he said, "I think I've been praying for you! I've been looking for someone interested enough to attend the conference and then take the lead in finding ways to get the men of our church involved in Promise Keepers."

> ### *Bud had always prided himself on being an analytical and rational person. But now he found that what he'd believed in his head for years was somehow touching his heart.*

Bud literally backed away, held up a hand, and said, "Hey, I was just asking! I'm really too busy to consider going."

But Connie, who'd never heard of Promise Keepers before, urged him to look into the conference. "Why don't you at least call my brother Larry and ask what he knows about it?" she said. "He lives just a few miles from Boulder. Maybe he's heard something."

So Bud called Larry, who had heard lots of good things about Promise Keepers from several men in his church who had gone the year before. "If you came, I'd go with you," he said.

Bud quickly agreed. And he and Larry joined 50,000 other men at the University of Colorado football stadium, in a blistering sun and scorching 104-degree heat, for the two-day conference.

Larry was concerned about how the brutal heat might affect Bud. Larry himself sometimes sought shade at the stadium's edges and backside. But throughout the conference, Bud seemed oblivious to any physical discomfort, perhaps because he was so excited about what he found himself a part of. From the opening words of the conference, Bud was totally absorbed. The deep, rugged, rumbling resonance of 50,000 male voices lifted in songs of worship and praise moved Bud like no other music he'd ever heard. And one after another, the conference's major speakers somehow singled him out in that massive crowd to address his heart directly.

The drama began in the opening session on Friday night, when speaker Greg Laurie challenged the men to be sure they were trusting in Jesus as their Savior. It wasn't good enough, he said, that they attended church regularly, or even that they were at this conference. Only a commitment of their lives to Christ would bring them into God's family, give them the power to live as true Promise Keepers, and assure them of an eternity in heaven.

As Bud listened, he realized, *I've never done that. In all these years of going to church, reading the Bible, and everything else, I've never really given my life to Christ. I need to do that, and tonight's the night! Thank You, Lord!*

A few minutes later, when Laurie asked the men who wanted to commit their lives to Christ to come down in front of the stage, Bud turned to Larry and said with conviction, "I need to go down there." Larry gave him a huge smile and a bear hug, and then Bud got out of his seat and joined the river of men working their way forward.

As he reached the open area in front of the stage, Bud saw that it was filling rapidly with men who, like himself, were ready to make the most important decision of their lives. They came and came, hundreds and thousands of them from every part of the stadium, until the area was packed. The men were smiling and crying, hugging and shaking hands.

A counselor walked over and gathered Bud and a few other guys. Then he reviewed quickly the steps to faith in Christ and asked each man if he had any questions. Next, Laurie asked the throng of men to kneel as he led them in a prayer of confession and commitment. Bud knelt with the others, quietly repeating Laurie's prayer even as he thought, *This is the best thing I've ever done. I've never been so sure of what I needed to do.*

But that was only the beginning of Bud's transformation that weekend. When other speakers challenged men to personal integrity and purity, Bud compared his own standards to those of Christ and prayed, "Lord, I know now that I haven't come close to being a godly man in the past. I need Your help to raise and pursue a higher standard from this time forward. Please guide me and give me strength."

When speaker Howard Hendricks called for men to commit to the concept of spiritual mentoring, saying every Promise Keeper needed a Timothy in his life to disciple, Bud thought immediately of his son-in-law Andy, his stepdaughter's husband. When Hendricks also said that every Promise Keeper needed a Barnabas to help hold him accountable, Bud and

Larry turned and looked at each other. In the instant their eyes met, they both knew, without saying a word, that they would be each other's Barnabas.

And as various speakers called for Christian men to make a difference in the world around them, Bud caught the first glimpse of what God just might be able to do through him. *More men from our church have got to come here next year,* Bud thought. *If I tell them what God has done for me this weekend, they'll want to come, and He'll get a hold on them the way He's doing for me.*

Because he had never experienced anything to compare with the personal Rocky Mountain spiritual high he'd found in Boulder, Bud wanted desperately to share all his impressions with Connie. "It was incredible!" he told her. "The music, the speakers—everything! I just know God wanted me to be there."

Connie seemed not merely interested but genuinely inspired by his excited descriptions of the conference. Yet Bud couldn't help wishing she'd been there to see it for herself, because mere words, no matter how many or how passionate, just couldn't communicate the depth of what he'd witnessed and felt. So he vowed to show her over the coming weeks and months that he was a changed man. He also decided that when he got home, he was going straight to the staff at WABF to tell them he wanted to become a point man for Promise Keepers. His goal would be to recruit as many men as possible to attend a Promise Keepers conference already scheduled for Anaheim the next spring.

But no sooner did Bud get back to California than he developed an itchy, blistery rash that ran in a five-inch-wide band around the right side of his waist from the middle of his back to the middle of his stomach. He immediately went to the doctor, who told him it was one of the worst cases of shingles he'd ever seen.

Soon the rash began to fade, but as it did, the itchy discomfort was replaced by excruciating pain. It felt as if someone were repeatedly stabbing him with long, jagged shards of broken glass. Night and day it went on, week after week, physical agony such as Bud had never experienced. Medication did little to dull the pain, and the doctors could offer even less in the way of encouragement. They told Bud there was no way to predict how long his pain might last. It could ease up and be gone almost immediately, but they'd known patients with shingles who had suffered neurological pain for months and even years. Hearing that, Bud determinedly told Connie, "I have the feeling this pain may be something I'll just have to deal with the rest of my life."

Incredibly, Bud still never missed a day on the job. But what seemed even more amazing to Connie and the people around Bud was that despite the debilitating physical suffering and the overwhelming workload facing him every day at the office, Bud immediately set about living up to the commitments he'd made to God and to himself in Boulder. He clearly intended to be a true Promise Keeper, and nothing was going to stop him.

He soon made a lunch appointment with his pastor, Lee Eliason. Within minutes of taking their seats, Bud had moved the conversation beyond the usual weather-and-sports level of casual guy-talk to ask what was going on in his pastor's life. "We almost didn't make it to the salad bar that day," Lee recalled later. "I sensed a genuine interest on Bud's part. He clearly wanted to know what made me tick. So I answered him as honestly as I could, telling him what I was struggling with at that time as a man and as a minister. He listened with careful attention, exhibiting supportive empathy."

For the first time, Bud told Lee about his lymphoma. "How do you feel about that?" Lee asked.

"The uncertainty hanging over my future may be the worst of it," Bud answered. "I've got a great wife and a whole new depth of love for her, and it would be harder than ever to say good-bye to her."

"But you also have a greater appreciation for how much God loves her and will take care of her if you're not there," Lee suggested.

"That's right," Bud said with certainty. "And that's partly why I'm so turned on about Promise Keepers. I want to see other men get set on fire at one of their conferences the way I was. I want them to have the same assurance—not to mention the same sense of purpose—that I have now."

Lee was impressed by the changes in Bud and his obvious dedication to God and his family. "But perhaps the most significant result of this new relationship I was developing with Bud Schaedel," Lee said, "was the sense of his personal commitment and support for me. As we got ready to leave, he asked if he could pray for me, and I really felt lifted into God's presence by Bud's sincerity."

That lunchtime conversation was not a one-time occurrence, either. In the months that followed, whenever Bud saw his pastor, he would ask Lee how he wanted Bud to pray for him. And in church meetings, Bud would regularly say, "We need to pray for our pastor." When a group of men began praying with Lee before every service, he remembers, "It was such a humbling, gratifying, and empowering experience—unlike any I'd ever had in my years of ministry. Not only was Bud there for me as a personal friend and encourager, but his example and prodding inspired a movement of men to pray for me and support me in a way I believe played an important part in a revival which then took place in our church."

At every possible opportunity in church, Bud wanted to talk about Promise Keepers and the upcoming conference. In one men's meeting, someone said, "Wouldn't it be great if we could get 50 men to go?"

Bud's response was, "Surely we can do better than that!"

"What about 100 men?" another proposed.

"No, higher!" Bud urged.

The agreed-upon target was eventually 150 men. But everyone got the idea that Bud wouldn't be satisfied until every man in church had signed up.

Sometimes it seemed he was out to recruit the entire world. At his own expense, he bought and duplicated countless tapes sampling the music, message, and spirit he had experienced in Boulder. He would buttonhole friends, casual acquaintances, and even a few visitors before and after church, give them a videotape, and make them promise to watch it and pray about going to the Anaheim conference.

Everyone got the idea that Bud wouldn't be satisfied until every man in church had signed up.

And Bud didn't limit his recruitment efforts to church. He handed out tapes to people at work, where he'd never before been open about his faith. "The first time I talked to Bud on the phone after his trip to Boulder, he told me a little about his experience, and I sensed he was a changed man," recalls Bob Ripley, an executive from Bud's company's corporate headquarters. "I'd just finished Chuck Colson's book *The Body,* so I bought Bud a copy and sent it to him."

Bud called Bob to thank him for the gift and to tell him he was sending a tape of the closing session of the Boulder conference. "This is something you just have to get involved in, Bob," he said. "In fact, they're going to be coming out your way for a conference next summer in Indianapolis. And you've gotta promise me you'll go."

As the weeks stretched from summer into fall, Bud and his brother-in-law Larry talked regularly on the phone about their deepest feelings and concerns. Larry, who'd been a small-town police chief, was going through a discouragingly long and difficult stretch between jobs. So Bud spent most of their time on the phone trying to boost Larry's spirits with assurances of his own concern and prayers and reminders of God's faithfulness.

At home, Bud worked at strengthening his immediate family commitments. "Bud had always been fairly affectionate with his daughter and with mine," Connie said. "But I saw a greater tenderness with them and a new expression of physical affection with the boys." There was an easy openness in Bud that hadn't been there before.

After 20 years of marriage, Bud's unconditional love for Connie had so changed her life that she says she thought, *There's no way to improve on perfection.* But God's standards in a husband proved higher than hers. "As close as we always were," Connie says, "as much as we always shared, professionally and in our marriage, when Bud came back from that conference in Boulder, we moved to a level of intimacy far deeper than we'd ever known. We began to share on a whole new spiritual plane."

Then, during that fall of 1993, Bud's lymphoma returned. This was much sooner than his doctors had expected. Another round of chemo began in January 1994.

When Larry learned Bud was going into treatment, he wrote him a letter:

> Dear Barnabas: . . . I have some things I want to say to you. These last few years, especially this last one, have been the most trying times of my life. I want you to know what an inspiration you've been to me. If someone were to look up the word *perseverance* in the dictionary, they should see a picture of you. Whenever I thought I couldn't take another disappointment, I thought of you and your behavior through your ordeal, and I would find the courage to face another day. Just knowing you were there as my safety net gave me the ability to move forward and not stand still in despair. . . . For you to show your love and support for me and mine while you suffered so yourself is beyond my understanding. Thank you, Barnabas.
>
> There are three things I know. Connie loves you. God loves you. And we love you. Please, if ever I can do anything for you, call on me. I wish I could make all things better for you. You are in my prayers.
>
> Love, Barnabas Also.

Bud was in a lot of people's prayers during those months of chemo. Yet few knew how sick he was, because he still didn't talk about himself or his suffering. He also kept on working, taking off at noon for his therapy with a new doctor at a hospital close to home.

Through the entire ordeal, Bud continued to recruit more people for the Anaheim conference in May. To enable some men to go who couldn't afford the registration fee, the Schaedels set up a scholarship fund.

During this same time, Bud told Pastor Eliason he wanted to be publicly baptized. He looked weak and pale that morning standing in the baptistery next to his pastor. But when asked when it was that Christ became real to him, Bud boomed out his answer loud and strong. He told briefly how he'd first heard of Promise Keepers and decided to go to the conference in Boulder. His voice breaking with emotion, he said, "It was there on my knees with 50,000 men that I prayed to accept Christ into my heart for the first time."

After that public confession of Bud's faith, Lee baptized him. It was one of the happiest days of Bud's life.

As Bud intensified his efforts to sign up more men for the Promise Keepers conference, the chemo began to take its toll on his health. One of the dangers of chemotherapy is increased susceptibility to infection. So when Bud spiked a 104-degree fever, Connie tucked ice packs under his arms and rushed him to the emergency room. The doctors examined him and sent him home. His fever came down, but he experienced such severe sweats that Connie had to change the sheets three or four times a night. On a Thursday night when his temperature shot up yet again, Connie rushed Bud into the hospital, only to be sent home once more. On Friday he got another chemo treatment, and the following night he grew so feverish and delirious that he fell and opened a gash on his head. Connie sped him to the hospital, but they were sent home again.

On Monday, Bud called the doctor to explain that he was extremely ill and to demand an immediate appointment. The doctor's staff agreed only to move up a scheduled appointment from Thursday to Wednesday. By midweek, Bud was so weak that Connie had to put him in a wheelchair to get him to the doctor's office. His blood pressure had plummeted to 70/48. Bud had suffered kidney failure. He also had a blood infection that sent his blood count skyrocketing. The doctor admitted him to the hospital immediately.

The seriousness of Bud's situation was clear to anyone who walked into his room. For those visitors who had last seen him at church or at work just the week before, his sudden deterioration was shocking. Yet his spirits remained high. When someone commented about how hard life can be, Bud responded, "Life isn't so hard. It's just a boot camp for heaven." And he continued to talk to visitors about Promise Keepers.

On Thursday, Connie asked the doctor if things looked serious enough for her to call Bud's children. The doctor said that if it were his family, he'd call them. So she did, and the children made reservations to fly out the next morning. Thursday afternoon, Bud's breathing became so labored that he was moved to intensive care and put on a respirator.

Once the tube was inserted down his throat, there was no more talking for Bud. He had to resort to communicating by touch. But when the president of the church's men's group arrived that night, Bud excitedly held up 10 fingers. Connie had to interpret: "Bud wants to tell you that we've decided to fund 10 scholarships to the Promise Keepers conference. So on Sunday he wants you to announce that there's no reason for anyone to decide he can't afford to go."

That was Bud's last message to the world outside his family. He had done all he could to give as many men as possible the opportunity to experience Promise Keepers. By Friday morning, he was no longer conscious. And in the early hours of Saturday morning, Bud Schaedel died.

On the following Tuesday at Bud's funeral, several men from WABF paid tribute to him. Amid his own remarks, Pastor Eliason read the "Barnabas letter" Larry had sent Bud. And he showed a video of Bud's baptism so that Bud gave his own testimony to those who'd come to his funeral.

After the service, a gentleman came up to Connie and introduced himself as a local representative of the Promise Keepers. He said he knew it was a sensitive time, but he had been so moved by Bud's story that he wondered if Connie would give her permission for it to be told as part of the Anaheim conference. Connie agreed.

Two weeks after Bud Schaedel died, in the closing session of the conference in Anaheim Stadium (the Big A), Lee Eliason was called to the platform. He told the men filling the Big A about coming to know Bud Schaedel, a man whose life had been changed at the Boulder conference less than a year before. He spoke movingly about the impact Bud's love and support had

had on him and his ministry. He showed a brief clip of the video from Bud's testimony at his baptism, and he told about Bud's death just 14 days earlier. He also explained how tirelessly Bud had worked those last months of his life to get men to the conference in Anaheim. Then Lee directed everyone's attention to a specific spot in the upper deck and asked the 250 men from WABF to stand in honor of Bud Schaedel.

The stadium erupted in applause that went on for almost a minute before Lee could be heard again saying, "I'd like to tell you one more thing about Bud Schaedel tonight." Then he recounted Bud's 20-year habit of bringing coffee and the "Love Is" cartoon to Connie in bed every morning. Lee went on to say how that example shamed him. "I'm going to miss my friend Bud Schaedel," he said in conclusion. "But tonight I'm honored to introduce a very special lady, Bud's widow, Connie Schaedel."

Once again the crowd of 50,000 men erupted in a standing ovation and cheers that might have startled the folks at Disneyland a mile or so away. For more than a minute, Connie stood at the podium, soaking in the over-whelming response and shaking her head in amazement. When the clapping and cheering and whistling finally stopped, she told that stadium full of men, "This is, indeed, an incredible honor. Bud was an exceptional husband, a good father, a man who liked to come alongside men and women of all races and cultures. He was a man of truth. And on top of all that, he had a wonderful sense of humor.

"That was the man I knew for 21 years. He was always a Promise Keeper in the making. Last year he went to Boulder with a very short prayer on his lips. He said, 'Lord, change my heart.' And indeed that happened. I didn't think you could improve on perfection. But the story got better as Bud became a complete and total human being—because he could finally express his love for the Lord and for other men, a side of him that had never fully developed.

"The explosion that took place in his heart last year in Boulder has provided incredible fallout for all of us who loved him—me, our family, his friends, our loving church. We all became Promise Reapers.

"Gentlemen, I just want you all to know . . . it works. Amazing grace fell on Bud last summer in Boulder. And it will fall on you."

Again the stadium exploded with cheers and applause that lasted long after Lee and Connie had walked off the stage.

The fallout from the final months of Bud Schaedel's life has continued. In the weeks that followed, Connie learned that through Bud's influence, a young man who'd worked for him had brought 10 men from his church to Anaheim, and a friend of that fellow's had brought 15 more from another church. A few weeks later, Bud's friend Bob Ripley led a group of 68 men from his church in Grand Rapids, Michigan, to the Promise Keepers conference in Indianapolis. In all, nearly 350 men attended Promise Keepers conferences in 1994 through Bud Schaedel's effort and influence.

Many of those men had their lives transformed, starting with Connie and Bud's son-in-law Andy. He went to Anaheim on the ticket Bud had hoped to use himself, and at that conference Andy made his own personal commitment to Christ. Bob Ripley reports from halfway across the continent how, as a result of Bud's influence, the lives of 68 men were forever changed—as was their church.

Some months after the conference, Connie met a man from her own church who confessed, "I, too, was at the conference in Boulder in 1993. But that last night, I wasn't ready to become a Promise Keeper. However, as I watched how God used Bud those last months of his life, I saw what a mistake I'd made. I've made that commitment myself now."

Perhaps Bud's brother-in-law and Barnabas, Larry, sums it up best when he says, "In Bud's life I saw a powerful example of how God can work through one person who is willing to make a total commitment to Him."

Personal Evaluation

If you could write your own epitaph, what would you like it to say? Why?

In the Group

1. What have you done since the last session to reach out to your world? What will you do in the next month?

2. Below are some possible reactions to the Bud Schaedel story. Check all that apply to you; then share your choices with the group and your reasons for picking them.

____ I'm inspired to try to be the same kind of husband.

____ I feel guilty that I'm not as good a husband.

____ I'd like to have the same kind of impact in my church.

____ I don't think I could have that kind of impact in my church.

____ I believe God can use me in a great way, though perhaps not exactly like Bud Schaedel.

____ I don't think God would ever do anything exceptional through me.

3. How did Bud go about trying to support his pastor? What can you do for yours?

4. In your own words, what were Bud's primary motivations after his experience at the Promise Keepers conference?

5. What one thing about Bud's story stands out in your mind as something you would like to emulate? Why?

My Response

Complete the following prayer, and then say it to God: "Almighty God, I want to be a Promise Keeper who raises the standard in his life every day. The biggest obstacle I see in doing that is _____

_____

By Your power, my first step toward overcoming that will be _____

_____

In Jesus' name, thank You for helping me to keep my promises."

Memory Verse

"I can do everything through him who gives me strength" (Phil. 4:13).

APPENDIX: THE REST OF THE STORY

One of the stories told earlier in this book was cut off at a certain point because we thought that giving you all the details there would get in the way of your own grappling with the issues involved. Because God worked in such a wonderful way, however, we now want to give you the rest of the story to His honor and glory.

A Promise Keeper Strives for Ethical Integrity

In the ethics story of Sergeant Harvey Mitchell, you'll recall that he was about to go back and help evaluate the unit that had gotten rid of him. At first, Colonel Webb, his old commander, objected to Harvey's presence on the StanEval team. But with God's help, Harvey bent over backward to be fair and objective. And in the end, Colonel Webb pulled Harvey aside to say, "I appreciate your integrity, Sergeant Mitchell. I wish your situation here had worked out differently. But it looks like things have worked out very well for you."

Harvey smiled and nodded. "Colonel Webb," he said, "I've just learned to let the Lord fight my battles."

A year later, Harvey received a request for a meeting from Sergeant Sherman, the immediate superior who had instigated Harvey's removal from the Fundamental Electronics school. At first suspicious, Harvey soon discovered that Sherman was having serious marital and career problems, and he had called Harvey because "you're about the straightest guy I know who walks with God."

Harvey was amazed, but Sherman, because of his difficulties, was open to hearing about the gospel! And that very day, John Sherman trusted in Jesus Christ as his Savior. The following Sunday, Harvey had the privilege of baptizing him.

"The entire church knew who he was," Harvey says, "so there was crying and praising God all through the congregation. They were seeing right in front of their eyes what happens when you let the Lord fight your battles. Sometimes He not only makes your enemies your footstools, but He may even save them and let you baptize them."

God still wasn't done, however. Another year later, Harvey found himself evaluating Major Zylinski, who had also participated in the injustice against Harvey. Zylinski was now retired from the Air Force and was working as a civilian instructor on the base. He was surprised and nervous when he saw who his evaluator would be, but Harvey was again able—with a lot of prayer—to be fair and objective.

At the end of their time together, Zylinski looked Harvey in the eye and said, "Sergeant Mitchell, I appreciate your fairness."

"When I went back to tell the guys in StanEval what had happened," Harvey says, "they couldn't believe it. They were laughing and shaking their heads, wondering what the odds were of my being assigned to evaluate Zylinski with all the hundreds of instructors out there on the base."

Harvey concludes, "I know it sounds incredible, but I've learned God doesn't care much about the odds. When I decided to let Him fight my battle for me, He went a perfect three for three."

ACKNOWLEDGMENTS

This book would not have been possible without the dedicated work of many people. Promise Keepers would like to recognize and thank them publicly for their efforts.

Kurt Bruner and his team—Jim Guffey, Brad Mazzocco, Earle Morgan, and Keir MacMillan—sorted through more than 8,000 letters and testimonies sent to Promise Keepers to identify those stories that might be worth telling in detail.

John Allen of Promise Keepers took hundreds of those letters and made initial calls to determine which few stories should actually find their way into the book.

Sherri Woods of the Focus on the Family legal department prepared contracts and documents necessary for the book.

Diane Eble called the subjects of the stories—as well as their wives, parents, children, pastors, and friends as needed—and conducted the in-depth interviews from which the stories were written.

Donna Goodrich transcribed all those interviews so the writer could make efficient use of them.

Gregg Lewis used his storytelling skills to bring those accounts to life and help readers grapple with the issues of raising the standard in their own lives.

Finally, as noted in the Introduction, the Promise Keepers advisory board wrote the chapter introductions, personal evaluations, group discussion questions, and "My Response" sections for each chapter. That board included John Allen, Dr. Rod Cooper, Dr. Gordon England, Jim Gordon, Al Janssen, Dr. Gary Oliver,

Pete Richardson, Dr. E. Glenn Wagner, Larry Weeden, and David R. White.

A special thanks to Susie Swenson of Promise Keepers and Lori LoCurto of Focus on the Family for typing, copying, arranging meeting rooms, preparing and sending FedEx packages, monitoring faxes, and relaying urgent phone messages between two very busy ministries.

ADDITIONAL RESOURCES AVAILABLE FROM PROMISE KEEPERS

BOOKS & STUDY GUIDES

Seven Promises of a Promise Keeper (Colorado Springs, Colo.: Focus on the Family, 1994). Also available on four 90-minute audiocassettes or five compact discs.

What Makes a Man? & Study Guide, Bill McCartney (Colorado Springs, Colo.: NavPress, 1992)

Focusing Your Men's Ministry, Peter A. Richardson (Denver: Promise Keepers, 1993)

Brothers! Calling Men into Vital Relationships, Geoff Gorsuch and Dan Schaffer (Denver: Promise Keepers, 1993)

Daily Disciplines for the Christian Man, Bob Beltz (Colorado Springs, Colo.: NavPress, 1993)

What God Does When Men Pray, William Carr Peel (Colorado Springs, Colo.: NavPress, 1993)

Strategies for a Successful Marriage: A Study Guide for Men, E. Glenn Wagner, Ph.D. (Colorado Springs, Colo.: NavPress, 1994)

What Is a Promise Keeper? (Denver: Promise Keepers, 1993). Available in audiocassette only.

WORSHIP & PRAISE MUSIC

Face to Face: Worship for Men, Maranatha! Music (Laguna Hills, Calif.: 1993). Available in compact disc, audiocassette, songbook, or words only.

PK Live: Worship Tape, Maranatha! Music (Laguna Hills, Calif.: 1994). Available in compact disc or audiocassette.

Seize the Moment: Worship for Men, Maranatha! Music (Laguna Hills, Calif.: 1994). Available in compact disc or audiocassette.

Promise Keepers: A Life That Shows, Sparrow (Brentwood, Tenn.: 1994). Available in compact disc, audiocassette, or songbook.

Raise the Standard, Marantha! Music (Laguna Hills, Calif.: 1995). Available in compact disc or audiocassette.

For more information regarding resources and conferences, please write to:

Promise Keepers
P.O. Box 18376
Boulder, CO 80308

The Power of a Promise Kept is also available on compact disc or audiocassette.

If you or your men's group has not yet gone through it, we also highly recommend you obtain **Seven Promises of a Promise Keeper.** That book lays out the foundation of the Promise Keepers ministry, and it's designed to be used in much the same way as this one. It's available on compact disc or audiocassette as well. You can get these resources from Promise Keepers or your favorite Christian bookstore.

<u>My Notes, Prayers, and Commitments</u>

My Notes, Prayers, and Commitments

My Notes, Prayers, and Commitments

<u>*My Notes, Prayers, and Commitments*</u>

<u>*My Notes, Prayers, and Commitments*</u>

<u>My Notes, Prayers, and Commitments</u>

<u>*My Notes, Prayers, and Commitments*</u>

My Notes, Prayers, and Commitments

<u>*My Notes, Prayers, and Commitments*</u>

My Notes, Prayers, and Commitments

<u>My Notes, Prayers, and Commitments</u>

<u>My Notes, Prayers, and Commitments</u>

My Notes, Prayers, and Commitments

<u>My Notes, Prayers, and Commitments</u>

<u>My Notes, Prayers, and Commitments</u>

<u>My Notes, Prayers, and Commitments</u>

<u>*My Notes, Prayers, and Commitments*</u>

<u>My Notes, Prayers, and Commitments</u>